ADMINISTERING GRANTS, CONTRACTS, AND FUNDS

ADMINISTERING GRANTS, CONTRACTS, AND FUNDS

Evaluating and Improving Your Grants System

David G. Bauer

With Contributions by Mary L. Otto

American
Council on
Education

NEW YORK
Collier Macmillan Publishers
LONDON

Macmillan
Publishing
Company

Copyright © 1989 by American Council on Education and
                    Macmillan Publishing Company,
                    A Division of Macmillan, Inc.

Macmillan Publishing Company
866 Third Avenue, New York, N.Y. 10022

Collier Macmillan Canada, Inc.

Library of Congress Catalog Card Number: 88–38027

Printed in the United States of America

printing number
1   2   3   4   5   6   7   8   9   10

Library of Congress Cataloging in Publication Data

Bauer, David G.
    Administering grants, contracts, and funds : evaluating and
improving your grants system / David G. Bauer ; with contributions
by Mary L. Otto.
        p.   cm.—(The American Council on Education/Macmillan series
on higher education)
    Bibliography: p.
    ISBN 0-02-901951-6
    1. Corporations, Nonprofit—United States—Finance. 2. Research
grants—United States. 3. Corporations—United States—Charitable
contributions. 4. Public Contracts—United States. 5. Fund
raising—United States. I. Otto, Mary L. II. Title. III. Series:
American Council on Education/Macmillan series in higher education.
HG4027.65.B38   1989
658.1'5224—dc19   88–38027
                                                                        CIP

Contents

Preface

Nonprofit organizations face great challenges for survival in the 1990s. Not since some benevolent soul started the not-for-profit movement has the existence of nonprofits been so precarious. In the search for dollars, the grants and contracts area will play a major role in survival for many. For others, grants and contracts will actually contribute to the demise of the organization, for without a careful analysis of the effect grant dollars have on influencing the mission and purpose of an organization, the benefits of external support can have a negative impact.

Most books on grants administration deal with the legal aspects of handling funds and suggest appropriate accounting techniques. This book encourages the reader to look at the more complex and important questions regarding grants administration in its entirety.

In order to increase the ability of an office of grants and contracts to play a positive role in your organization, it pays to consider the various functions outlined in this book.

Introduction

There are approximately 1,000,000 nonprofit organizations in the United States. Approximately 350,000 are considered grant or gift supported. Seeking outside funding through the grants mechanism is a necessity to these 350,000 nonprofits and a great opportunity for the remaining 650,000.

A large percentage of these nonprofit groups utilize the grants mechanism to:

- expand existing programs and research

- develop and implement new program areas

- supplement costs of operation and services

- replace and acquire equipment

- build and repair facilities

- add to and train staff

The marketplace for grants to fund these and other needs is constantly changing. The federal grants marketplace has fluctuated from 40 billion in 1980, to 22 billion in 1983, to over 30 billion in 1989.

Foundation grants have grown consistently in spite of fluctuations in the stock market, recessions, and inflation. The year 1987 saw foundation grants increase by almost 8.4% to 6.38 billion. While 1987 and 1988 stock prices slowed stock market growth and growth of foundation portfolios, foundation monies available through grants continue to increase.

Corporate grant making is expected to experience a reduced rate of growth in the late 1980s compared to the strong increases experienced in the early part of the decade ($2.359 billion in 1980 to $4.5 billion in 1987). The 7,419 corporate mergers occurring in 1985 and 1986 further insulated the corporate board room from local community concerns and slowed corporate grant making.

However, the 11 billion dollars in foundation and corporate grants disseminated in 1987 and the 30 billion in federal grants are conservative estimates for the 1990s. Foundation, corporate, and federal grants will continue to grow.

Despite the enormous pool of available grant dollars, competition to win these dollars will heighten. Preliminary research suggests that as the number of applicants for funding increases, grantors will consider only those grantees who appear the most capable of fulfilling their proposal promises. Applicants who have successfully performed previously funded projects will continue to receive grants, but the number of first-time or new awards to organizations and project investigators with little or no track record will be reduced, making grants to organizations and individuals within a given category highly competitive.

Whether you are inexperienced or experienced, it is evident that you will need a superior grants system to compete for the resources. For example, in the private grants marketplace of foundation funding, payments in grants by the nation's 4,400 largest foundations increased 22.3% in 1987, while the number of grants increased by only 6.6%. In other words, those that had previously received funding got more. got more.

Larger and more successful nonprofit groups will find that in order to maintain an advantage over their competition they must:

- increase the credibility of their organizations

- reduce the element of error in the grants process

- increase efficiency of the proposal generation process

- improve their proposal writing skills

As funding sources become more knowledgeable, they will ask more sophisticated questions. For example:

- How does this proposal relate to the mission of the organization?

- Is this the "right" organization to fund?

- Why should this organization receive the grant instead of another organization in the same field?

- How does matching this particular organization with this grant meet our needs?

This book is designed for use by a variety of nonprofit organizations—large and small, experienced and novice. The principles of sound, sponsored project administration are the same regardless of the background of the grantseeker. This book may reinforce efforts that you already have undertaken, or it may encourage you to examine new areas of improved or expanded grants administration. Each chapter of this text is designed to prompt you to:

- consider the points presented in the chapter

- analyze how applicable the techniques are to your grants system

- develop a work plan to assist your organization in making the changes you deem desirable

- prepare you and your grants office to deal with changes in the grants marketplace

You may give the numerous worksheets and checklists provided in this book to your key staff, director, or president of the board in order to make an independent assessment of your organization's performance in each of the areas suggested by the chapters. This will assist the experienced grants office in evaluating its existing structure as it relates to these areas, identifying areas that could be improved and areas in which performance is adequate.

Remember, to reinforce positive grantseeking behaviors in your staff, and to isolate those areas and behaviors needing improvement, you need concrete evaluation based on performance. By employing the techniques suggested in this book, you will develop an expanded view of the services a grants office can and should perform.

May you use the techniques and processes outlined in this book to support, change, and expand the worthy causes that your organization represents.

CHAPTER 1

The Purpose of the Office of Grants and Contracts Administration

The genesis of this book was my twelve years of experience in grant consulting and grants-effort process audits. A grants-effort process audit consists of an in-depth analysis of an organization's grants mechanism and a plan for improving its efficiency through identifying weaknesses and enhancing strengths. Through my experiences, I have learned that each grants office is unique.

The office that administers grants and contracts has many names, and the role of this office is far from standard. In some cases, the role of the grants office varies according to the personality and interests of the director or administrator. However, there are certain functions that a majority of grants offices have in common, as well as certain functions that are left unaccounted for or performed haphazardly and inappropriately.

The grants office can promote the mission of an organization and provide great returns irrespective of whether it's identified as the Office of Grants Administration, the Office for Sponsored Projects, or the Office of Research and Development. If you establish the goals and objectives for the office's performance, the results will be dramatic.

Review the goals and objectives of your grants office, and consider adding any of those from the following list. Involvement in these areas will determine the need and usefulness of your organization's grants office.

- development of opportunities to further the goals of the organization through grants, projects, research, and programs funded by sources outside of the organization

- promotion of an atmosphere conducive to developing and sustaining interest and involvement in grant proposal preparation and support activities by staff

- protection and enhancement of the integrity and image of the organization through management and monitoring of communication with funding sources

- provision of information on the use of matching funds and in-kind contributions allocated to the grants process

- insurance of the integrity of sponsored project funds, and assistance in interpretation and compliance with funders' rules, regulations, and wishes so that both legal and ethical requirements are met

- analysis of the grants marketplace and the provision, to management, of funding information needed in fiscal and program decisions affecting the organization

- provision of leadership in impacting the grants marketplace and increasing funding opportunities for the good of the organization, its projects, clients, and benefactors

- development of grant strategies on marketplace trends that provide for a mix of grant funds from federal, state, foundation, and corporate sources

At this point, you may want to review the table of contents. Each chapter is derived from or related to the broad goals that have just been listed.

Many administrators are unsure of the role that they want the grants office to fulfill because they do not know what the office can do. Through completion of the checklists at the conclusion of each chapter, you will develop a description of your grants office. Your office's description should be tailored to the individual needs of your organization. The varied size and scope of your agency and what you want from an organized grants effort will vary and may even change as your organization develops.

List the established goals and objectives of your grants office on the following worksheet. You may also wish to ask a sample of individuals from your organization what they think your office's purpose is. Another good activity is to give selected individuals your list and ask them to put the items in order of priority.

Meeting the Mission of the Organization through Grants

Without a mission statement or case statement to provide direction to an organization, the grants effort cannot play an effective role in helping to achieve the goals of the organization. Yes, that old, dusty document that is used only at five-year planning time—the mission statement or case statement—is critical to the grants effort. This statement of the purpose of your organization will enable you to:

- evaluate the extent that funding sources will be attracted to your established mission and institutional goals

- set realistic criteria for judging what grant direction to embark upon

- determine criteria for the use of matching fund requirements and in-kind contributions

Many organizations have an entrepreneur type of grant writer on their staff. I had one that I refer to as "Dr. No Problem." Dr. No Problem would announce that he had discovered a "pile of grant money" that he had to apply for immediately, if not sooner. His record of creating pandemonium within our nonprofit organization was overlooked because he brought in lots of money and was a nice person who meant well. Closer examination revealed that his actions had major drawbacks.

Money can be the worst element to add to a nonprofit organization. A desperate need for money may be a warning sign that the organization is no longer focusing clearly on the problem or need it was created to address or that the need has changed and that people no longer view the organization and its programs as viable. Even if the weak financial state of the organization can be attributed to other causes, such as poor fiscal decision making, the temptation to go after any and all money creates a problem if the additional funds move the organization further from its mission.

4

GRANTS OFFICE GOALS/OBJECTIVES WORKSHEET

Please list the established goals and objectives of your grants office.

1. _____
_____
2. _____
_____
3. _____
_____
4. _____
_____
5. _____
_____
6. _____
_____
7. _____
_____

Please list any other goals and objectives that you think your grants office *should* have.

1. _____
_____
2. _____
_____
3. _____
_____

Producing a proposal to acquire a "pile of grant money" is advisable only when the project fosters the mission or case statement of the organization. Any activity that does not foster this purpose, no matter how innocuous it seems, keeps the organization from moving toward its goals and may change or subvert the organization's mission.

While changes in the mission and the pressure of finances may be causative agents of change for an organization, they should be controlled through a conscious decision-making process. Grant funds should be pursued by premeditated measures.

Executive directors should not be bullied into sponsoring projects because they do not want to be accused of not seeking all available funds or appear as if they are restraining the entrepreneurial staff member. Remember, a devoted staff member who is well intentioned will not mind relating grant opportunities to the predetermined interests of the organization.

Your Case Statement or Mission Statement: Who You Are

You may ask, "What has my organization's mission or case statement got to do with getting a grant?" The answer is *everything*. Your case statement consists of how and why your organization got started and where you are going in the future.

1. How and why did your organization get started? What were the social problems or reasons for starting your organization? Societal need today is more valuable than the number of years your organization has been in existence. In fact, one funding source remarked to me that the organizations she had the greatest doubts about were those that have been around for a long time. She felt that older organizations were generally too bureaucratic and had a tendency to lose sight of their mission or purpose. She believed that some were here today because they were here yesterday.
2. Where is your organization going in the future? Your case statement should include a five- or ten-year plan, or both. Funding sources want to place their projects with grant winners who will exist in the future.

Your case statement also allows you to examine what you are doing today. Have you deviated from the past? Why? What effect

MISSION/CASE STATEMENT WORKSHEET

1. Past: How and why your organization got started
Year _____ Prime Movers/Founders _____
Societal Need _____
_____

2. Present: Changes from original mission _____
_____

Societal-Need Changes _____
_____

Current Priorities _____
_____

Who are our clients, and who do we benefit now? _____
_____

What are our staff needs? _____
  Additional Staff _____
  Training of Staff (in-service, motivation, etc.) _____

What are our facility needs (buildings, renovations, improvements, equipment, etc.)? _____
_____

3. Future: Where your organization will be five years from now
Changes in Mission _____
_____

Societal-Need Changes _____
_____

Changes in Staff _____
Changes in Facilities _____
New Areas (Service Areas, Research Areas, Extension of Programs, etc.)
_____
_____

has time had on your mission and reason to be? What are your current priorities, programs, clients, staff, buildings, and unique characteristics?

Show the funding source that your organization is worthy of funds and that the project it has invested in will continue to benefit people because you have planned on it.

If your existing case statement is not relevant to today's directions and problems, then update it regardless of your decisions and plans for your grants office. Begin the process of updating your organization's case statement by brainstorming ideas with members of your organization. Rules for brainstorming are addressed in the next section.

The Essentials of Brainstorming

One of the best techniques for developing ideas is to brainstorm with your staff, board, volunteers, and advisory committees. In addition to fostering involvement in your organization, this technique has the added benefit of capitalizing on the group's collective genius. Support is built for the ideas since others were invited to share in their generation. The project or solution becomes a group project, and everyone is more willing to work to make the idea become a reality.

Brainstorming is a simple technique that quickly generates a long list of creative ideas and solutions to problems.

1. Ask individuals to form groups of five to eight people.
2. Appoint a neutral group leader to facilitate the group process and task. This individual should encourage and prod other members, check the time, and so on.
3. Appoint a recorder. This individual will write down all ideas generated and can be the facilitator.
4. Set a time limit. Ten minutes is more than enough for each area. Five minutes will keep the process going at a fast pace.
5. State one question or problem. What are our current needs (staff, buildings, renovations, improvements, equipment)? What changes will be needed in the future in programs areas, clients, and so on? What changes will be necessary in terms of buildings, equipment, and so on to accommodate future program changes?

    Changes in facilities include renovations, new buildings, and equipment. Changes in staff include additional staff, training needs, and in-service areas. New areas include service areas, client population, research areas, and program extensions.

6. Ask group members to generate as many answers to the question as they can within the time limit.

7. Encourage group members to piggyback on each other's ideas. *Piggybacking* is suggesting a new idea that adds to one already given.

8. Record all answers. Combine those that are similar.

Two important rules to remember are:

• Avoid any evaluation or discussion of ideas until the process is over.

• The recorder can ask to have ideas repeated, but no comments by others are allowed (e.g., "We can't do that," "That's stupid," or "I disagree").

Take time to discuss each idea or suggestion. For example, if you have ten ideas, two minutes per idea for explanation and questions will consume twenty minutes of group time.

Since your list can be prioritized later, do not get too concerned with an idea that group members may want to focus on. When you use a voting system, as suggested in Chapter 2 of this book, you will eliminate or weaken any ideas that the group does not hold in high esteem.

Developing a Mission Statement for the Grants Office

The grants office is directly responsible for assisting the organization in dealing with its current priorities and in preparing for the future. The organization's mission or case statement can be reorganized to provide the grants office with direction and to shape its role in the organization's plan.

The Mission or Case Statement Worksheet can be developed into the plan for the grants office. Using your answers from questions 2 and 3 on the worksheet as a guideline, ask yourself what you would do if your organization received a large check (e.g., 10 percent of your organization's total budget) in the mail. The money was sent by an anonymous benefactor and can be used for anything. Using the Wish List Worksheet, brainstorm a list of present uses with your

WISH LIST WORKSHEET

Your organization has just received a check for $ _____ (10 percent of your organization's total budget). The money was sent by an anonymous benefactor and can be used for anything.

Brainstorm and list ideas for its *present* use.

1. _____
2. _____
3. _____
4. _____
5. _____
6. _____
7. _____
8. _____
9. _____

Using this money, or part of it, brainstorm and list any changes you would make in the *future* in programs, facilities, staff, etc.

1. _____
2. _____
3. _____
4. _____
5. _____
6. _____
7. _____
8. _____
9. _____

staff, the board, and selected advisory committees. Also, brainstorm a list of changes you would make in the future in programs, facilities, and staff. Keep a record of the projects and areas for investigation you have developed through your brainstorming.

Note that the establishment of these projects and areas for investigation is not intended to severely limit the staff's innovative ideas or freedom. It merely helps the staff to know what the areas of interest are so that they can come up with creative solutions and techniques that can be applied to these areas. The staff may as well know in advance that a very good approach that has nothing to do with the list of areas that need to be addressed might not be supported. Disseminating a published list to staff members is a positive step that avoids explanations and problems later on when a project is not supported.

The role of the grants office is to assist the organization to meet present needs and to prepare for future needs by securing external funds that will move the organization toward its goals. The remainder of this book is designed to provide you with the knowledge of the services that most grants offices provide in seeking to meet the mission of an organization.

Do you need a grants office? Can you afford a grants office? Can you afford not to have a grants office? These questions are yours to answer.

GRANTS OFFICE INVENTORY
Chapter 1
The Purpose of the Office of Grants and Contracts

For Each Activity/Item Listed, Check Status:

Activity/Item	Reviewed, Appropriate Part of Grants Office	Reviewed, Appropriate Part of Other Office (List)	Reviewed, Not Applicable	Reviewed, Inappropriate Needs Action	Non-existent, Needs Action
1. Mission statement for organization 2. Goals and objectives for grants office					

Complete this Section for Each Activity/Item Needing Action:

What Needs to Be Accomplished? (Activity/Item)	By Whom? (Office/ Person)	By When? (Time Frame)	Resources, Required— Personnel, Supplies, Equipment, Programming, etc.	Estimated Costs

CHAPTER 2

Measuring the Success of Your Grants System

The success and efficiency of an organization's grants system is dependent upon the criteria used for evaluation. Without understanding the purpose of a grants system, it is impossible to evaluate its success. For example, can you identify which of the following examples describes a successful grants system?

- A grants system that brings in twice the amount of external funds compared with other organizations of similar size and staff background

- A grants system that is so fiscally accountable that every audit substantiates superior grants accounting and generates praise from the funding source

- A grants system that consistently operates within a narrow time frame from the conception of an idea, researching of funding sources, and production of a proposal. This system utilizes computers to provide researchers with funding-source application data instantly and produces budgets, time lines, and proposals with computer speed and accuracy

These examples can be evaluated only on the subjective criteria that is implied or mentioned in each description (e.g., speed, accuracy, etc.). None of the examples have to do with meeting the mission or purpose of the organization through the grants system. In fact, many nonprofit organizations do not evaluate their grants system by its ability to move the organization toward its mission or purpose. When meeting the mission or purpose of an organization is ignored as the primary indication of success, the result is a grants effort evaluated on the mechanics of the grants process, such as:

- how quickly and thoroughly the grants office handles requests for funding-source information

- the amount and quality of assistance the grants office provides in writing, editing, budget development, typing, reproducing, and delivering the proposal

Lacking criteria on which to evaluate the functions of a grants office leads to evaluation of the technical assistance that most grants offices provide or the more common measure of success of the grants system: *money.*

Asked to describe the grants effort at their nonprofit organization, most administrators will be quick to relay the total amount of grant support in dollars, or they might make a reference to the success rate or number of proposals funded as compared with the number submitted. These two commonly referred to "indicators of a successful grants effort" may have little to do with moving the organization toward its predetermined mission or goal.

Preparing proposals *solely* aimed at meeting the funding sources' needs may be counterproductive to the goals of the grant-seeking organization. In fact, it may be wise to eliminate a grants office if the organization's resources are being used to seek out funding for *only* those projects that have the least risk of rejection and the greatest promise of money. If a grants office's only goal is to amass a great amount of money and develop a high success rate, it may be:

- subverting the original mission of the organization

- using space for nonmission-related projects

- altering the focus of the staff and board

In the hustle and bustle of the grants world, the tendency to "follow the money" is an ever-present danger. Predetermining why your organization is doing each particular project is an important component of a truly successful grants system that works for the organization.

However, on occasion, a nonprofit organization may have to take a less-than-optimum path to move toward accomplishing its mission. When the available funds to move in the predetermined direction are limited, nonexistent, or highly competitive, a proposal may be written and a grant accepted to help with overhead and to stay in business. However, if funds are attracted to nonpriority areas too often, the mission of the organization will become blurred and eventually abandoned.

The purpose of this chapter is to assist you in assessing the grants potential of your organization and developing a plan for grants success.

Establishing the Goals of Your Grants Office

The key to evaluating the success of your grants office lies in your efficiency in identifying and securing the best funding sources and grant programs for your organization. The "best" sources and programs are those that provide your organization with a bright future, ensure your organization's credibility as a grantee, and move your organization toward meeting its mission.

To measure the success of your grants office you must establish its goals. To do so, locate the list of organizational needs developed in Chapter 1, and rank-order the list. By rank-ordering the list, you will help focus your entire organization's efforts. In addition, you will be able to analyze the list and determine which priorities the grants process will assist in achieving.

Remember that the grants effort may be used to attract some or all of the components of a priority. For example, a list of priorities for the grants office of the Department of Pediatrics at the University of Rochester School of Medicine and Dentistry included:

- improving the department's capacity for accomplishing more bone-marrow transplants and research

- developing a focus on research of AIDS in children

- providing a means for parents in an eleven-county region to remain close to their hospitalized children

A ranking process revealed that providing a means for parents to remain close to their hospitalized children was the number one priority because it was a component of several other priorities. The result was a concentrated effort to provide grant support to construct a Ronald McDonald House.

If the priority of the grants office had been to accumulate as much money as possible, and money had been the sole criterion for evaluating the efforts of the grants office, it might have been wiser to invest staff time and effort into securing bone-marrow and/or AIDS research grants. However, reaching our organizational mission and the prioritization of our projects were the measurement criteria, not the total amount of grant dollars secured.

- What are your organization's priorities?

- What parts or steps to meeting these priorities can your grants effort affect?

- What grant-related projects take precedence over others?

RANK-ORDERING ORGANIZATIONAL NEEDS

Rank-ordering the list of needs developed in Chapter 1 will assist you in prioritizing your grants effort. Rank-ordering can be done in a group setting or individually. In many cases, the individual rank-ordering process is preferred so that anonymity can be maintained and group pressure controlled. Through the rank-ordering process you will arrive at a "weighted" list of priority areas. Use the following rank-order procedure or develop your own.

Send the participants in the process a list of the priority areas or needs of the organization and request that they rank them numerically with "1" as their highest priority (first choice), "2" as their second priority (second choice), and so on. Provide direction and focus by reminding participants that they need to review the list from the organization's perspective, and not their own, and that they should keep in mind special considerations, such as space and equipment needs, that may be necessary to accomplish the priorities. You may find it helpful to use the following Priorities Worksheet.

SCORING SYSTEMS

The following methods of scoring may assist you in interpreting the choices on the Priorities Worksheet.

1. Count only those areas that are listed in a certain segment of the rank order. For example, count only the top ten items on each worksheet. Give an item one point each time it appears in the top ten. Then list the items in rank order from highest to lowest.
2. Take the highest scoring item on each worksheet and do another rank order with those items only, or take the top ten areas

PRIORITIES WORKSHEET

The following areas have been identified as priorities for this organization. Please assist the grants effort by rank-ordering the listed areas. The area you assign number 1 to will be your first choice. Your number one choice should be the area you feel is most important to seek grant funds for. The area you assign 2 to will be your second choice, and so on.

Area	Rank order
_____	_____
_____	_____
_____	_____
_____	_____
_____	_____
_____	_____
_____	_____
_____	_____
_____	_____
_____	_____
_____	_____
_____	_____
_____	_____
_____	_____
_____	_____
_____	_____
_____	_____
_____	_____

developed from method one and resubmit them for a second rank-ordering. This will force the participants to focus on those areas that their peers also voted for and will eliminate any focus on nonpriority or pet projects.
3. Give each participant in the process a certain number of total points to distribute to the listed items. After everyone has distributed their points, add the total points awarded to each area. This will allow you to easily develop a rank-ordered list. The more total points, the higher the priority.

This activity can be accomplished in a group. The Priorities Scoring Worksheet at the end of this section allows up to sixteen areas to be listed in the left-hand column. Points for each individual are allocated in each person's column, which is designated by the individual's initials. The total points should be listed in the total points column to ensure that everyone has the same number of points to allocate. Total the points to the right, and you will arrive at the total points for each area. Use the last column on the right to develop the rank order of the areas. The area receiving the greatest number of points will be number one, the area receiving the second greatest number of points will be number two, and so on.

Please note that if you are sending the participants the list to complete as an individual activity, you do not need to send the worksheet to them with every other participant's score. Send a separate list of items and combine the scores to develop the group scores.

Analyzing and Determining Your Grants Potential

You can make an educated guess or estimate of your organization's grants potential with reasonable accuracy. The potential is a function of the following factors:

- the amount of grant money available (1987 figures),
    federal funds ($33+ billion)
    local and state funds (varies by area)
    foundation support ($6.38 billion)
    corporate support ($4.5 billion)

- the fundability of your projects as related to your organization's mission: how unique, how creative, how replicable, and the other variables funders look for

PRIORITIES SCORING WORKSHEET

ORGANIZATIONAL NEEDS/ AREAS IDENTIFIED	INITIALS								TOTAL POINTS PER AREA	RANK
Individual Scores										

- your organization's geographic location and overall image in the nonprofit field

- your staff, their expertise, and their fundability

How much grant money is available? Approximately $45 billion was granted in 1988. This does not include corporate contracts to nonprofit organizations, government contracts, or funds from the Department of Defense. Local and state grants and contracts that are not a result of revenue sharing or the pass-through of federal grants are also not included. The total marketplace is difficult, if not impossible, to calculate and understand. A review of the introduction is recommended to increase insight into the marketplace.

- Estimates are that federal grants for 1988 will be about $33 to $35 billion.

- In 1986 foundation support increased by 20.41 percent to $5.2 billion, while 1987 saw growth rise at a rate of 8.14 percent.

- Corporate grants rose drastically in 1985 but leveled off in 1986 to $4.5 billion and continued to stay level at $4.5 billion in 1987.

The $45 billion awarded in 1988 was given to hundreds of thousands of the one million nonprofit organizations seeking funding. Whether your organization will receive a portion of next year's funds will depend on many factors.

The ability to attract grants is dependent on the quality of the projects that your organization generates. Whether your projects are model projects, research projects, demonstration grants or replications of existing projects, they must demonstrate quality ideas. What is important is the degree to which the projects chosen meet the needs of the funder as well as move your organization toward attaining its mission.

By reviewing a list of the projects that a prospective funding source has supported, you will develop knowledge of how good your project will look to the grantor.

Chapter 6 outlines techniques that will assist you in procuring a list of grantees and possibly a sample proposal to assist you in evaluating your project's chances. By analyzing the funding-source data, you will know if your project is too costly for the grantor and how and when to separate your project into fundable components. In general, you will begin to develop an eye for fundability.

Your organization's geographic location and reputation in your area is another important funding factor. Your organization must look good to the funder. Obviously, the term *good* is relative and can be defined only by the prospective grantor.

Some government granting programs are directed toward a specific group, for example, Young Initiator Awards, grants for Strengthening Developing Institutions (colleges and universities), and postdoctoral fellowships. Prospective grant seekers can review applicant eligibility and categorical guidelines to determine in what grant areas your organization may fit the criteria of the funder.

You can research potential funding sources to determine what types of organizations appear on the funded list and then compare them with your organization. Remember that not all federal grants go to the biggest and best-known nonprofit organizations, although ten colleges and universities account for over one half of the allocated funds. An analysis of who gets the grants will provide you with valuable insight. You will be able to determine how changes you make in your organization's image will affect your fundability. You will learn how to increase your marketplace potential by developing consortia arrangements with the winners. Consideration should also be given to the grantee mix that some government funding sources seek to maintain. The ratio of large, small, well-known, and unknown grantees can be determined only by a review of the list of the past grantees.

Contact with the funding source may reveal interest in your organization and your project even when there is a mismatch in image or type of organization. A representative of a funding source once remarked to me that he had never had a proposal from an organization like the one I represented and was therefore very interested in our application.

An analysis of government grants and the types of nonprofits that are successful in attracting them reveals the following information. Government grants from the largest granting agencies are directly correlated with two things: the number of individuals in the nonprofit organization who have Ph.D.'s or engineering and other terminal-research-related degrees; and the amount of money that the organization's state attracts in federal research dollars. The state you are located in is a general indicator of your marketplace. Developing your staff, increasing your linkages and consortium projects, and increasing your staff's ability to produce more quality proposals will have some impact on these hard, cruel facts—but not much.

Analysis of the recipients of government grants also reveals that some of the states that do not show up as leaders in attracting government grants from several agencies or even one federal agency turn out to be leaders in attracting federal grant dollars in specialty areas. For example, Vermont was not one of the top ten states to receive National Institutes of Health (NIH) awards in 1987, unless you look at subspecialties and discover that it had a leadership role in one specific area. Striving to become a leader in attracting funds to a specialty area, rather that making a shotgun attempt at all grants, may improve your potential.

After analyzing your staff and your state's position in your field, select an organization similar to yours (either currently or at a certain stage in your development) and review federal lists of grantees to see how many and what types of grants the organization received. Copies of one or two funded proposals, obtained on a trip to Washington, D.C., will provide you with the vitae of key staff members. This will assist you in determining how to build a staff that can compete. Since many proposals contain lists of equipment, dedicated space, and support staff, you will be able not only to analyze your government grants potential but also to develop a cost-effective plan to move toward that goal.

I am currently assessing the potential of my department of pediatrics to attract grant funds for research and demonstration projects. By briefly reviewing the grants awarded to the leading institutions in the field, surveying the vitae of several staff people who have worked at the top three organizations, and searching for grant areas that the big names are not known for, I have put together a list of ideas and a compilation of our equipment and personnel. The grants resources I will use to position us for success are available, but not in my department. By selecting an area that we can compete in, we will maximize our potential and chances for success.

Private foundations may provide a degree of hope for the smaller or less well known organization. An analysis of 990-ARs (Internal Revenue Service forms) shows that many foundations fund nonprofits with appealing projects or unique solutions with little regard for organizational image and/or stature. A sincere commitment to solving a problem and a record of integrity can carry an organization a long way.

However, do not be too idealistic or confident. A recent survey of foundations revealed that while their award dollars had risen by 22.3 percent, the number of new recipients increased by only 6.6 percent. These numbers may indicate that funders feel more comfortable giving more of their money to known entities and grantees, thus making it difficult for the new grantee to enter the marketplace.

Use the computer-based research services available in your library or at the Foundation Center Library to identify several sources that have funded projects in your field of interest.

Review the list of past grantees carefully. Who were the chosen organizations? What is their image? Will you look good to the funding source? A recent survey of grants made by 444 of the 24,589 foundations demonstrated the importance of performing a survey of funded projects by geographic location of the grantee. Six states received 60 percent of the awarded funds.

The next variable to consider in developing your fundability equation is your staff's expertise. The background of the individuals who generate the project and their ability to carry it through are important to funding sources.

A review of competitive federal research grant recipients reveals a profile of the acceptable project director (PD) or principal investigator (PI). While some government programs will designate grants for "young or new" investigators, designations get more confusing as investigators have "some" experience and may be known in their field. The question is, are they known well enough to receive a federal grant? I have worked with many well-educated and intelligent researchers who develop a project in an area they are not well known in and spend valuable time fighting a system that does not value the research or project idea as much as *who* is doing the work. Unfortunately, many organizations hire consultants to get them a grant when the reality of the situation is that the key staff members involved in the project are not known well enough in the field to be awarded support. A review of the list of successful grantees and contact with the funding source concerning the background of the proposed staff are strongly advised.

The following materials are recommended to assist your staff in objectively analyzing their grants readiness: the Winning Grants Self-Assessment Worksheet, the Grant Winner Worksheet, the Winning Grants Time Line, the Winning Grants Systematic Approach Worksheet, and the Winning Grants Plan for Improvement.

The first two worksheets (Grant Winner and Self-Assessment) are designed to provide staff with a method to assess their position in the field and to allow them to develop insight into their productivity in terms of those indexes of involvement most frequently used in the grants/research field. By using these materials, individuals can analyze their own fundability.

You can use the results of this analysis in a variety of ways. One way is to compare your project personnel with those who worked on a previously funded grant. If your grants office has obtained a copy of a funded proposal, your prospective grant seeker may compare his or her fundability with that of the successful project director or principal investigator through an analysis of the biographical sketch or curriculum vita in the funded proposal. This process will reveal your prospective grant winner's strengths and weaknesses. The comparison of key project personnel may lead the project director to secure letters of endorsement or develop arrangements with other investigators to build staff fundability.

The two self-assessment worksheets—Grant Winner Worksheet and Winning Grants Self-Assessment Worksheet—can also be used to begin the process of setting personal goals. A good idea is not enough to get a grant. Researchers *must* publish, present, attend meetings, and so on. These exercises develop an awareness of the competitive grants game.

The Winning Grants Self-Assessment Worksheet helps users develop insight into their areas of past research, new areas of interest, and life-style and to determine how these factors are related to grants competitiveness. Questions one through three are designed to identify those individuals with whom the proposed grant seeker studied. This review can also include fellow students and others who have since become involved in research.

Questions four and five deal with the proposed researcher's professional and personal life-style. Research requires time, including time to read the relevant literature and time for the other factors noted on the worksheet. Since the would-be grant seeker typically has not developed the life-style and time-management skills of a successful grant seeker, he or she must determine what personal decisions and forces in his or her life impede progress.

The Winning Grants Plan for Improvement Worksheet ties the previous two assessment tools together by asking the participants to list what "action steps" they will take as a result of their self-analysis. In my seminars, I copy the Winning Grants A Systematic Approach Worksheet on two-part carbonless paper. I carefully review questions one through three and encourage workshop participants to review the other self-analysis tools. In this way they can determine the personal objectives and the action steps that they need to take to increase their chances of being funded.

By analyzing the resources needed, participants can also calculate the cost of their personal development. Those who have made it their objective to receive funding or a certain score by reviewers can develop action steps such as:

- getting to the office one hour earlier for one year and using the extra time to read X number of research articles in their grants field

- joining the appropriate professional organizations and attending regional and national meetings

- developing a grants-review committee to examine past proposals in an area and brainstorming funding strategies

- searching through the literature to determine the status of those individuals they studied with in terms of their publications and grants they've received

The Winning Grants Time Line encourages individuals to list their activities or action steps and draw them on a time line that represents when the activity will begin and end. Calendar months are listed in the top of the twelve columns; the first column represents the month that the individual is performing this exercise.

If the Systematic Approach Worksheet has been completed on carbonless paper, you can encourage the participants to place one copy in an envelope, seal it, and address it to themselves. Your grants office will then mail the copy to each participant after an agreed-upon period. I return self-made agreements after sixty or ninety days. This concept, known as a *self-learning contract,* is designed to encourage the self-change and self-direction that your staff must undergo to be successful researchers.

GRANT WINNER WORKSHEET

1. Number of research articles I have read within the last two years

   _____   0
   _____   1– 5
   _____   6–10
   _____   11–15
   _____   16–20
   _____   21 plus   estimate _____

2. Number of conferences and/or major meetings I have attended within the last two years

   _____   local   _____   regional
   _____   state   _____   national

3. Number of articles I have submitted for publication within the last two years

   _____   0
   _____   1– 5
   _____   6–10
   _____   11 plus   estimate _____

4. Number of articles I have had published within the last two years

   _____   0
   _____   1– 5
   _____   6–10
   _____   11 plus   estimate _____

5. Number of books I have had published within the last five years

   _____

6. Number of chapters I have contributed to textbooks within the last five years

   _____

7. Number of presentations I have made within the last two years

   _____   local   _____   regional
   _____   state   _____   national

8. Postdoctoral work I have completed within the last five years

   _____

9. Within the last five years:

   fellowships:
      applied _____   received _____

   stipends:
      applied _____   received _____

   scholarships:
      applied _____   received _____

   sabbaticals:
      applied _____   received _____

10. Number of grants applied for within the last two years

   _____   0
   _____   1– 5
   _____   6–10
   _____   11–15
   _____   16–20
   _____   21 plus   estimate _____

11. Number of grants I obtained funding for within the last two years

   _____   0
   _____   1– 5
   _____   6–10
   _____   11–15
   _____   16–20
   _____   21 plus   estimate _____

12. Number of consortium arrangements (grant related) I have been involved in within the last two years

   _____   0
   _____   1– 5
   _____   6–10
   _____   11 plus   estimate _____

SELF-ASSESSMENT WORKSHEET
MY UNIQUENESSES, STRENGTHS,
AND AREAS TO IMPROVE

1. Area(s) of thesis and dissertation:

2. People I studied under (advisers, professors, thesis/dissertation committee members, etc.) in graduate school:

3. Areas of interest other than thesis and/or dissertation areas (i.e., new areas of interest):

4. Key factors that will assist me in developing a plan to become more involved in the grants area and research (e.g., changes in life-style, changes in work style, shifting of time commitments, reallocation of priorities):

5. Major factors that will keep me from becoming more involved in the grants area and research:

PLAN FOR IMPROVEMENT

1. Review Winning Grants Self-Assessment Worksheet. If you are still interested in your dissertation area or other areas of past work, how can you update your knowledge of the field(s)? For example, what can you read to bring you up-to-date?

2. Make a list of past advisers, dissertation committee members, mentors, and professors who worked with you or who continued research or interest in your area of study. Contact them through your former department, alumni office, or colleagues. Review data bases to uncover research articles and research in progress by these individuals. List any current interest areas of yours that relate to those uncovered in your search.

3. If you are no longer interested in the specific area of your past work, what are your new areas of interest? If you are unsure, what can you do to determine areas of interest? For example, brainstorm possible fields to study, list potential research ideas and questions of interest, etc.

4. Develop a plan to address each of the items on the Grant Winner Worksheet. How will you increase your participation in each of the activities? Put your grant winner's action plan on a self-learning contract.

WINNINGRANTS

A Systematic Approach

David G. Bauer Associates Inc.

OBJECTIVES / ACTIVITIES • ACTION STEPS •   RESOURCES NEEDED   LIST KEY PERSONNEL NEEDED

WINNING GRANTS:

Copyright 1988

David G. Bauer Associates Inc.

Consulting Services

TIME LINE

ACTIV-ITY NO.												

GRANTS OFFICE INVENTORY
Chapter 2
Measuring the Success of Your Grants System

For Each Activity/Item Listed, Check Status:

Activity/Item	Reviewed, Appropriate Part of Grants Office	Reviewed, Appropriate Part of Other Office (List)	Reviewed, Not Applicable	Reviewed, Inappropriate Needs Action	Non-existent, Needs Action
1. List of organizational priorities 2. List of priorities of the grants office 3. Criteria to evaluate the functions of the grants office 4. Activities/materials to assist staff in analyzing "fund-ability"					

Complete this Section for Each Activity/Item Needing Action:

What Needs to Be Accomplished? (Activity/Item)	By Whom? (Office/Person)	By When? (Time Frame)	Resources, Required—Personnel, Supplies, Equipment, Programming, etc.	Estimated Costs

CHAPTER 3

Developing a Preproposal Review System

Most proposal-generating nonprofit organizations have a proposal sign-off procedure (see Chapter 8) to ensure that all responsible administrators are aware of the commitments and obligations that they will have to take on if the proposal is accepted and the funds are granted. It is quite surprising to find that most of these same organizations do not use a system of preproposal signatures to symbolize endorsement and signing on to the potential commitments that will be seen later at the sign-off time.

Preproposal review allows your organization to control and monitor the grant-seeking process in a proactive manner. Having a proposal sign-off procedure with no sign-on component is analogous to having an airport with strict landing requirements and rules but no take-off regulations. The organization is letting anyone represent it in grant seeking while having little or no control or knowledge of the grant-seeking overtures.

Consider the following advantages of a preproposal review system.

1. A preproposal review system coordinates the grant seeker's initial interest in seeking funds with that of the grants office and fosters a proactive grants system that reinforces forethought and an organized grants effort. This organized effort contrasts with the last-minute proposal-development efforts produced when reacting to deadlines only.

2. A preproposal review system reduces the chances that several grant seekers from your organization will contact a funder with no knowledge of the others' efforts. An organization's image as a well-managed and responsible prospective grantee is damaged when the funding source is subject to several unorganized or haphazard contacts from the organization that indicate that the "grants homework" on the funding source has not been done. Although entrepreneurial grant seekers may be well intentioned, they can make serious mistakes that can result in a poor image of your organization and lessen your future credibility with funders.

In a case in point, a college president and his grants person were caught off guard when visiting a foundation to explain a major college grants initiative. The foundation director remarked that he was very interested in an idea proposed by Professor Goodwriter from their college. When the president looked surprised and confused, the foundation director explained that Professor Goodwriter had just left his office one hour ago. The director was quite surprised that the professor, the president, and the grants person had not traveled the 250 miles to his office together. The president, demonstrating superior presidential qualities, remarked, "You mean *former* Professor Goodwriter, who used to be at my institution?" But in spite of the humor, the damage had already been done. Most likely, the foundation director had already begun to question the institution's fiscal controls and the integrity of its grant-seeking system.

A preproposal review system will provide "traffic control" so that funding sources receive a clear, organized image of your organization's management system and grant-seeking priorities.

3. Preproposal review will ensure the efficient use of your staff's time. The requirement that a grant seeker must seek approval before approaching prospective funding sources guarantees that he or she will not waste time pursuing a funding source or a proposal idea that would not receive your organization's final approval. In one instance, I worked extensively with three professors on a health-related training grant. I checked with administrative officials verbally over one part of the project that might evoke controversy and received a tentative approval. When the proposal was circulated for final approval and signature (sign-off), it was decided that it might encourage other proposal writers to use a similar approach, and while the proposal was not necessarily improper, it could not be submitted. The proposal was already at the print shop. Fifteen copies had partially been produced, and the four of us had spent many, many hours working on it. It would be a long time before I would see another proposal from those professors.

The fact that I did not have anything in writing and that the administrative officials developed selective amnesia and did not recall my original conversation persuaded this institution to develop a preproposal review system. When the preproposal sign-on procedure was introduced, the faculty had no problem accepting it. The system required that the administration approve all proposal concepts in advance and indicate, in writing, any special conditions that must be met for final approval.

4. A preproposal review system allows the organization to evaluate the relationship between its mission and the proposed grant. Since every grant requires the allocation of space and a commitment by the staff, it is imperative to address how the organization's mission will be met by the proposed activity. Even if the proposed project is *totally* supported by the funder, the question of whether it is appropriate in meeting the mission must still be addressed. The process of preproposal review is even more crucial if the proposal calls for matching funds or in-kind contributions.

Grants can actually subvert the mission and move an organization away from its goals and objectives. The temptation of grant seekers to "go for the gold" at the expense of an organization's mission has steered many not-for-profit organizations away from their purpose and caused confusion in the board and staff.

From the viewpoint of the prospective grant seeker, preproposal review is insurance that final sign-off, allocation of grants-office support, and approval for matching funds will be forthcoming.

5. Preproposal review may also include an assessment of the quality of the proposed project. A committee may be formed to review the idea that the proposal is based upon and offer suggestions for improvement and alternatives for locating and securing funds.

This preliminary review can be followed by a more extensive review when the proposal is fully developed and the funding source identified.

The $2.3 million profit-making corporations in the United States would never allow individuals representing them to interest a potential buyer in a product that *may not* even be produced by the corporation. Yet in the not-for-profit grants field, individuals contact funders without the knowledge of the organization and attempt to interest them in supporting (buying) a project that has not been approved by the organization.

While most nonprofit administrators would agree that reasons to develop a preproposal review system are convincing and compelling, few have a system in place or are willing to initiate one. Many feel that asking grant seekers to participate in another procedure would be a waste of time since many cannot even get their completed proposals signed off in a timely fashion; others believe it would not be right to ask grant seekers who are investing their "spare" time in the grants pursuit to complete another form. However, I strongly suggest that you consider implementing a preproposal review procedure to evaluate and improve your grants system. You may use the following Preproposal Review Form, or a variation of it, to assist you in your efforts.

The Preproposal Review Form can be tailored to fit your organization's needs. More space may be necessary to outline the solution, protocol, or approach to the problem. You may use this form as a cover sheet briefly explaining the project, and attach another page describing the protocol.

The purpose of the form is to obtain a "license" to "hunt" for funding sources. It is your administration's responsibility to make comments in the left-hand margin of the form. This is the administration's opportunity to outline concerns or conditions that the grant seeker must address or be aware of to be eligible for a final review and sign-off.

This form should be circulated to the administrators who may have valuable advice or who must sign off before submittal. The section at the bottom of the form designates those projects that will not be endorsed under any circumstances (rejected) and those that must meet certain conditions before they will receive endorsement (e.g., space is a problem, so the project must be done out of the facility).

This sheet should then be returned to the prospective grant seeker so that he or she will be aware of any and all limiting conditions that must be dealt with in the grant-seeking process.

The reviewing official in your organization should receive a copy of this form with the final sign-off sheet so that he or she can see the original comments. Although meeting the considerations that were originally identified should result in official sign-off and endorsements, it is important to remind grant seekers that special circumstances may cause a proposal that was originally approved to not receive final sign-off.

PREPROPOSAL REVIEW FORM

This form is designed to give the potential proposal writer insight into the administration's feelings concerning the appropriateness of this project, the amount and type of resources that will be committed to it, and an indication of any areas that will need to be addressed to secure final signature at the time of submittal.

Comments

Problem Area:

Solution:

Relationship of Proposal to Mission/Purpose:

Project Director(s):

Duration of Project:

Funding Sources to Be Approached:

Nonpersonal Resources Needed:
  Equipment:
  Supplies:
  Facilities/Space:
  Other:

Personnel Resources Needed:

Position	*% of Time*	*Salary/Wages/Fringes*

Matching Requirements/In-Kind Contributions:
  Money:
  Staff:
  Space:
  Equipment:

TOTAL MATCHING/IN-KIND CONTRIBUTION:

TOTAL AMOUNT REQUESTED FROM FUNDING SOURCE:

( ) ACCEPT proposal as outlined.
( ) ACCEPT WITH RESERVATIONS. Conditions must be met as listed in Comments section.
( ) REJECT. Idea is unacceptable and will not be supported under any circumstances.

Name of Reviewing Official:

Signature of Reviewing Official:

Date:

GRANTS OFFICE INVENTORY
Chapter 3
Developing a Preproposal Review System

For Each Activity/Item Listed, Check Status:

Activity/Item	Reviewed, Appropriate Part of Grants Office	Reviewed, Appropriate Part of Other Office (List)	Reviewed, Not Applicable	Reviewed, Inappropriate Needs Action	Non-existent, Needs Action
1. Pre-proposal review system • "sign-on" sheet or preproposal review form • preproposal review committee					

Complete this Section for Each Activity/Item Needing Action:

What Needs to Be Accomplished? (Activity/Item)	By Whom? (Office/Person)	By When? (Time Frame)	Resources, Required—Personnel, Supplies, Equipment, Programming, etc.	Estimated Costs

CHAPTER 4

*Developing Staff
Interest in Proposal
Development*

Why do individuals write grants? What motivates your organization's staff to get involved in the hassle of proposal preparation?

I have always been motivated by the grants opportunity. The prospect of using someone else's money to do what I've always wanted to do, or to meet my organization's needs, was real enough for me to pursue grants. However, not everyone views the opportunity to become involved in grant seeking with the same enthusiasm.

I asked the participants in one of my Winning Grants seminars to complete the following sentence: "When I hear the word *grants* I think of _____." The words used to complete the sentence included *rushing, deadlines, panic, chaos, burning the midnight oil, heart attacks, audits,* and *rules.* With this negative image of the grants process, it is a wonder that individuals become involved in this area.

When grant involvement is included in part of an individual's job description, or required for tenure, grant-seeking activities can be understood. But what about the thousands of individuals who get involved in grant seeking without being "forced" to? What motivates these people?

Grant administrators often tell me that they are not concerned with what motivates the grant seeker since their job is to administer grant funds, not procure them. However, I point out that there would be no funds to administer if proposal initiators decided not to get involved in the highly competitive grants system. The grants system is dependent upon individuals who get involved, and everyone

37

involved in the support of this system should be sensitive to the reasons that grant seekers perform as they do. By examining the psychological theories of Abraham Maslow and Frederick Herzberg and applying these theories to grant involvement, you may be able to assist your grants office in developing a better understanding of your organization's staff.

Maslow, in his hierarchy of needs theory, might say that individuals become involved in grants because:

- their security is threatened;

- they have a need for social approval, to belong to a group, and to feel they are a part of a greater good;

- they desire esteem, self-respect, and the respect of others;

- they desire the maximum development of self and to achieve their highest potential (self-actualization).

Grant writing may result when an individual's security is threatened. In this instance, possible deprivation may move the individual to action. For example, when grant success is an employment requirement, staff members may work out of a sense of threatened security. However, it is estimated that most of the people in our country have their basic needs met and, therefore, would probably not need to resort to proposal preparation to maintain their security needs. Only those who would be released from their jobs if grant funds were not obtained would be threatened.

Our need for social approval, to belong to a group, and to feel that we are part of a greater good may also spur some of us to become involved in the extra work of proposal preparation. The growth in the number of nonprofit groups, and the hours that are volunteered to their causes attest to the fact that most individuals in the United States reach this level. This would explain some of the so-called selfless work done for the good of others. The desire to belong to a cause or group is also a strong motivator, and not-for-profit organizations build upon this desire by providing a focus to help the less fortunate and/or joining together to expand understanding and knowledge in a particular field. Both the motivation for social approval and the desire to serve others lead to a greater good while satisfying the need to belong.

The desire for esteem, self-respect, and the respect of others may also motivate people to produce proposals. This desire for self-esteem may explain why advocates and volunteers become involved in the grant-seeking process and invest large amounts of time with no remuneration. It may also be why faculty and staff who have positions that do not require involvement in grant seeking will invest their time and effort in the process and why the dissemination components of a grant are so important (publishing, speaking engagements at conferences, etc.).

The highest level in Maslow's theory is self-actualization—achieving potential within self, creativity, and the desire for maximum development of self. Few of us reach this level and since life is in a constant state of flux, this level is reached and then lost when an individual has a problem with one of the previously mentioned supporting levels. As much as we might like to think that self-actualization is the level of achievement and the ultimate motivation of most grant writers, the other levels probably have a greater influence on proposal development.

Note that money is not viewed as a motivator in Maslow's theory. Although remuneration can help to fulfill a person's security level, pay is not the reason that most individuals write proposals. More likely, the desire for respect, esteem, and self-actualization may be the key to why people put in the effort.

According to Herzberg's theory of motivation, the extra effort required to produce proposals may be derived from "motivators" or "satisfiers." Based on this explanation of human motivation, five environmental or "hygiene" factors must be provided for in the work setting. They include: policies and procedures, supervision, salary, interpersonal relations, and hygienic and pleasant working conditions. Individuals must know what is required of them. They must understand the role of supervision and the remuneration policies associated with the different standards of work. In addition, the work setting must allow for interpersonal relations with co-workers and offer facilities for bodily needs and functions.

Herzberg explains, however, that meeting these five needs *alone* does not necessarily result in superior performance. These factors act primarily as preventive maintenance. They must be provided for but do not necessarily provide the motivation or the satisfaction that is required to encourage superior performance. The motivators are:

- *achievement*—the opportunity to satisfy the need to achieve
- *recognition*—fulfilling the need to be rewarded through recognition for work
- *the actual work itself*—the opportunity to be involved in the field or area of work and the addressing or solving of the problem
- *responsibility*—the opportunity to be responsible for and in control of additional resources

- *advancement*—fulfilling the need to move up the organizational ladder

Examine the willingness of your staff to become involved in grants based on the motivational factors identified by Maslow and Herzberg. Examine their willingness to perform superlatively.

Please note that neither of these theories pinpoints money as a significant motivator. Furthermore, individuals do the extra work involved in grant seeking even though federal- and most state-funded grants do not allow project directors or principal investigators to be paid additional salaries or wages. If the grant requires the time of this key individual, he or she must be released from his or her normal responsibilities. For example, a full-time worker who allocates 50 percent of his or her time to a grant must be released of 50 percent of his or her former full-time job responsibilities. In addition, individuals prepare proposals in their spare time since most nonprofit organizations do not give them release time or free time to do so. Proposal development and the reasons to seek grants clearly lie in areas other than monetary remuneration.

When veteran grant seekers were asked why they seek grants, the responses included the following.

- Grants allow me to explore my areas of interest.

- Grant proposals help to move my organization toward its goals.

- Clients need the results grants generate, such as equipment, therapies, research findings.

- A funded grant makes me feel important, needed, and powerful.

- I can get the things that my organization cannot afford to give me and my colleagues (e.g., equipment, secretarial assistance).

- Grants can lead to publishing, the deliverance of papers at professional meetings, and travel.

What techniques has your organization developed to provide your grant seekers with the components related to superior performance? Review the factors identified with high levels of motivation. Compare your present techniques and those suggested on the following Motivational Assessment Worksheet. Use this worksheet to help you assess and improve your grants environment.

MOTIVATIONAL ASSESSMENT WORKSHEET

List the factors that motivate your staff (social approval, esteem, recognition, achievement, etc.). List the techniques or activities currently used to increase staff motivation.

Motivators   **Activities**

_____   _____

_____   _____

_____   _____

_____   _____

_____   _____

_____   _____

_____   _____

_____   _____

_____   _____

Review the following list of techniques and activities useful in increasing staff motivation. Of these, are there any you are not currently using? Place a check mark next to those you will initiate.

_____ Awards Program—grants person of the month, year, etc.

_____ Recognition Program—plaques, stipends, dinner with board members, etc.

_____ Public Relations—external recognition through newspaper releases, pictures, publications, conference presentations, etc.

_____ Professional Recognition—recommendation for membership in prestigious professional groups, honorary societies, etc.

_____ Achievement Recognition—increase in status in organization: special parking area, flexible time, special purchasing power, increased budget, acquisition of new or limited-quantity equipment, etc.

GRANTS OFFICE INVENTORY
Chapter 4
Developing Staff Interest in Proposal Development

For Each Activity/Item Listed, Check Status:

Activity/Item	Reviewed, Appropriate Part of Grants Office	Reviewed, Appropriate Part of Other Office (List)	Reviewed, Not Applicable	Reviewed, Inappropriate Needs Action	Non-existent, Needs Action
1. Techniques/activities designed to increase staff motivation • award program • recognition program • public relations—external recognition • professional recognition • achievement recognition					

Complete this Section for Each Activity/Item Needing Action:

What Needs to Be Accomplished? (Activity/Item)	By Whom? (Office/Person)	By When? (Time Frame)	Resources, Required—Personnel, Supplies, Equipment, Programming, etc.	Estimated Costs

CHAPTER 5

Evaluating and Improving Your Grant Opportunity Research System

Your grants library and funding research system must be analyzed to determine its ability to support your current and future grants effort.

The age of computers has added a new dimension to what had been a library shelf of resource books on public and private funding sources. The library function of a grants resource center is only one component of a modern grants office. Establish the purpose and role of your grants office in providing information to your staff on funding opportunities and evaluate your system before you add intricate, expensive components.

Does or should your grants office:

- house funding source information for prospective grants seekers?

- disseminate a newsletter with funding source information?

- provide tailored funding research?

Developing and Evaluating Your Grants Information

DISSEMINATION SYSTEM

Computers have greatly enhanced your ability to locate funding sources and disseminate information on sources to your staff. Several data bases exist to assist your grants office and grant seekers. Some organizations develop and maintain their own funding-source data bases. The evaluation of several funding information and retrieval systems has led me to conclude that grants administrators make several assumptions concerning grant seeking.

- If a little information on funding sources for proposals is good, then a lot of funding-source information is great.

- The main reason that more of the staff do not prepare proposals for grants is their lack of knowledge of funding-source opportunities.

- Grant seekers would apply to more and different funding sources if they knew about them.

- A system tailored to produce proposal opportunities for specific areas of interest will increase proposal generation.

Many grants administrators make these assumptions, although they are usually not valid, and then push headlong into the grants-information dissemination business without evaluating their existing system. An evaluation will provide your office with the baseline data necessary to determine the success or usefulness of proposed changes.

The purpose of a grants-information dissemination system is to increase your staff's *sensitivity* to the potential grant-seeking holds for your organization and to make them *aware* that grant funds exist for their particular projects and interests.

The development of elaborate information systems may actually decrease proposal preparation and grant interest. Individuals are often reluctant to submit grant applications because they do not understand the process. If they feel that it is complex and difficult, they may experience cognitive overload when showered with newsletters and computer-generated lists of funding sources. In many grant systems the information on funding sources is poorly thought out and selected. Such information serves only to *reduce* the staff's sensitivity and awareness of potential funders.

To test the usefulness of an expensive funding-source alert system, I sent a brief profile of the funding source, including interests, application deadlines, and expected amounts of funds to be granted. I omitted the phone number and address of the funding source and placed a short note on the cover page instructing interested parties to contact the grants office for that information. The results demonstrated what I had feared. Those individuals who wrote proposals continued their work with little regard for the funding-source alert system. Their contact with funding sources that were currently supporting them and/or that had funded them in the past, and contact with other individuals in their field, provided them with most of their information; only a few of these grant winners asked for information on new or different funding sources. The rest of the staff—the majority—did not even request the information necessary to begin the grants process.

A survey of the staff concerning the usefulness of the funding-source information resulted in a very positive response. When confronted with the fact that no new grant seekers had requested the necessary information to initiate the grants process, most replied that to admit that they were not reading the information, or were not interested in grants, would be viewed negatively by the administration. Therefore, the administration was mistakenly confusing fear of reprisal for the need for more grant information.

To increase the probability that information on funding opportunities will be read and incorporated into the pursuit of grant funds, the information-dissemination system should be developed around the premise that only the most appropriate funding information should be presented to potential grant seekers. One way to accomplish this is through the use of a newsletter.

NEWSLETTERS

Many grants offices disseminate newsletters on funding opportunities to their staff. Some of these newsletters are simply photocopies of all or part of a commercially produced newsletter, while others are a sincere attempt to locate funding sources that are interested in their organization and its projects. The newsletter approach fulfills the need of the grants administrator to provide the potential grant writer with information on funding sources.

A generic newsletter for the entire organization that contains many funding sources and areas of grants interest forces the grant seeker to look at many unrelated funding sources. This can result in a waning of interest and an increase in the likelihood that the newsletter will be discarded. When your organization has multiple areas of interest, your objectives will be better achieved by producing several shorter, tailored newsletters. Each of your organization's areas of interest, programs, departments, or divisions could receive their own special newsletter. However, you may use the same cover page on each newsletter to develop the overall grants "spirit" of the organization. This cover page should be used for brief updates on new awards and pictures of projects and staffs and can also be used to highlight accomplishments, presentations, new equipment, and other improvements made possible by the organization's grants effort. The newsletter approach keeps the staff aware of the organization's progress toward meeting its mission while also serving to:

- increase awareness and interest in grants

- reinforce successful grant-seeking techniques (e.g., comment on how a preproposal contact was made)

- promote projects that have multiple area or division interests (e.g., announce that Sarah Jones is interested in a project in ____ and is looking for a coinvestigator from the ____ area)

- increase knowledge of the general grants marketplace (e.g., publish a brief summary of articles or research on corporate philanthropy in the local area)

- develop sensitivity concerning the success rate of awarded versus rejected proposals (advertise the monthly percentage of success)

- promote grants tips and successful techniques through a short section in the newsletter

- encourage your staff to become peer reviewers

These examples demonstrate how the grants newsletter can be developed so that it meets a range of needs of the grants office and the organization.

COMPUTERIZED GRANTS INTEREST PROFILES

In an effort to develop the most advanced information-dissemination system, many nonprofit organizations turned to microprocessors to provide the ultimate tailored retrieval system. The use of computers to obtain grant information has become popular primarily on college and university campuses, but many large nonprofits have now begun to use them as well. At first glance, a computerized retrieval system seems to far outweigh an inhouse newsletter in ability to provide individual grant seekers with funding-source information on specific areas of interest. But a closer look shows that a computerized system cannot serve as many purposes as an inhouse newsletter. For example, individual computerized profiles do not encourage communication between grant seekers or raise awareness of the grants effort or the organization's movement toward its mission. Review the multiple purposes of the inhouse newsletter to evaluate whether the individual computerized system is superior in promoting your total grants effort.

One large nonprofit organization I was employed by developed an elaborate system for logging the interests of staff members. Each staff member had to complete a seven-page questionnaire, and the information was then entered into a computer. The computer system held a comprehensive listing of both public and private funding sources. A monthly comparison match of staff interest areas and funding-source deadlines resulted in grant-alert announcements that were sent to staff members through the grants office. After several years the program was discontinued because it did not produce the proposals and interest in the grants mechanism that had been originally envisioned.

Until more data is developed and pre- and post-assessment is possible, we won't be able to fully evaluate the success of computerized profile and alert systems. In the meantime, you may realize greater results by having your grants coordinator meet with groups of potential grant seekers at faculty and/or staff meetings to ascertain areas of interest and then report back on potential funding sources.

GRANTS RESEARCH TOOLS

The following is a list and description of common research tools used by many grants offices to provide information on federal, foundation, and corporate grant opportunities. Complete ordering information for each entry can be found in the bibliography.

Please note that although various agency newsletters, requests for proposals (RFPs), guidelines, and annual reports are not individually listed, many federal agencies and foundations publish such items to inform individuals about the availability of funds, program accomplishments, and so on. These materials are available to the public upon request. The Grants Research Tools Worksheet will help you build a library of research material.

FEDERAL

- *Catalogue of Federal Domestic Assistance (CFDA)*—official information on all government programs created by law

- *Federal Register*—official news publication of the federal government that makes public all meetings, announcements of granting programs, regulations, and deadlines

- *U.S. Government Manual*—official handbook of the federal government; describes all federal agencies and provides names of officials

- *Federal Telephone Directory*—includes names, addresses, and phone numbers of federal government agencies and key personnel

- *Commerce Business Daily*—announces the accepting of bids on government contracts

- *Congressional Record*—day-to-day proceedings of the Senate and House of Representatives; includes all written information for the record

- *Federal Yellow Book*—a directory of the federal departments and agencies

- *Congressional Yellow Book*—a directory of members of Congress, including their committees and key staff aids

FOUNDATION

- *The Foundation Directory*—general information on thousands of the nation's largest foundations

- *The Foundation Grants Index*—cumulative listing of grants of $5,000 or more made by major foundations

- *The Annual Register of Grants Support*—provides information on all types of granting programs: foundation, government, and corporate

- *National Data Book*—directory of *all* the currently active grant-making foundations in the United States

CORPORATE

- *Corporate Foundation Profiles*—comprehensive data on large corporate foundations

- *The Corporate 500: Directory of Corporate Philanthropy*—provides information on the contributions programs of more than five-hundred large American corporations

- *The Corporate Fund Raising Directory*—provides information on the giving policies of several hundreds of America's top corporations

- *Annual Survey of Corporate Contributions*—sponsored by the Conference Board and the Council for Financial Aid to Education, this survey includes a detailed analysis of beneficiaries of corporate support

- *Dun and Bradstreet's Million Dollar Directory*—invaluable source of data on corporations with net worth of over $1 million

- *Standard and Poor's Register of Corporations, Directors and Executives*—up-to-date roster of the executives of major nationally known corporations

COMPUTERIZED DATA BASE INFORMATION RETRIEVAL SYSTEMS

- *Federal Assistance Program Retrieval System (FAPRS)*—a retrieval system that matches key words to federal granting programs (CFDA programs)

- *DIALOG Information Retrieval System*—Powerful online system with more than 100 data bases available

- *Sponsored Programs Information Network (SPIN)*—data base of federal and private fundings sources

- *COMSEARCH Printouts*—computer-produced guides to foundation grants published in the annual volume of *The Foundation Grants Index*

THE COMMUNITY GRANTS OFFICE

One function that your grants office may decide to perform is to provide a central grant-opportunity focus for the community.

The grant resources necessary to operate a grants library are expensive, and there is usually duplication of these tools within organizations and communities. Considerable savings could be realized by housing all of these resources in one area.

In addition to saving costs, the organization that sponsors a community grants library positions itself as a sharing organization. While

GRANTS RESEARCH TOOLS WORKSHEET

The following materials are basic to a grants office. Check off those items that you have currently available and those that you need to order. For those items that are currently available, list the location, edition and date of publication.

Available	Order	Material/Title	Location	Date/Edition
_____	_____	Catalogue of Federal Domestic Assistance	_____	_____
_____	_____	Federal Register	_____	_____
_____	_____	U.S. Government Manual	_____	_____
_____	_____	Federal Telephone Directory	_____	_____
_____	_____	Commerce Business Daily	_____	_____
_____	_____	Congressional Record	_____	_____
_____	_____	Federal Yellow Book	_____	_____
_____	_____	Congressional Yellow Book	_____	_____
_____	_____	The Foundation Directory	_____	_____
_____	_____	The Foundation Grants Index	_____	_____
_____	_____	The Annual Register of Grants Support	_____	_____
_____	_____	National Data Book	_____	_____
_____	_____	Corporate Foundation Profiles	_____	_____
_____	_____	The Corporate 500: Directory of Corporate Philanthropy	_____	_____
_____	_____	The Corporate Fund Raising Directory	_____	_____
_____	_____	Annual Survey of Corporate Contributions	_____	_____
_____	_____	Dun and Bradstreet's Million Dollar Directory	_____	_____
_____	_____	Standard and Poor's Register of Corporations, Directors and Executives	_____	_____

developing a college grants program, I surveyed the community for the grant resources that were available. Then I wrote a grant to a community foundation to purchase additional materials. When I finally received these new resources, I made them available to the community free of charge. Naturally, they were housed at my college grants office. Many nonprofit organizations came to my office to use the materials. Their visits often resulted in the sharing of ideas. Gradually these groups began to use our college staff in their proposals for curriculum assistance, help with evaluation of their projects, statistical assistance, training, and so on. The assistance we provided the nonprofit community groups was so well accepted that several asked us to provide more help. We encouraged these groups to sponsor a student assistant. The community group paid the tuition of the student (this was a state college and the tuition was low). In return, the student provided grants assistance at their site. Our grants office trained the student and maintained the library.

If the idea of sponsoring a community grants library appeals to you, review the following Letter Proposal: Area-Wide Grants Coordinating Office. You may tailor it to your organization and submit it to an appropriate local foundation or corporation for funding.

LETTER PROPOSAL: AREA-WIDE GRANTS COORDINATING OFFICE

The Need

Our area, like many cities across the United States, relies on its nonprofit organizations to provide many vital human services. These organizations depend on philanthropic support for survival and find it more difficult each year to raise needed funds.

However, the situation is far from hopeless. Grants support from foundations, corporations, and the federal government represents an opportunity for these organizations to dramatically improve their financial situation. Over $45 billion is granted by these three sources each year. Unfortunately, few agencies have the time, expertise, or resources needed to develop support from grants. A great opportunity is missed, and worthwhile programs go undone.

When they do apply for grants, local organizations often fail because their skills are not professional enough to face today's stiff competition for grant dollars. In many cases, grant failures can be turned into successes by training, more complete grant-research facilities, and attempts to create consortia projects sponsored by two or more local organizations.

We propose to develop an Area-Wide Coordination Office at _____ to fill these needs. It will be a conveniently located resource center for all grant-seeking organizations in and around the _____ area.

The Area-Wide Grants Coordinating Office will include a library of reference materials, files on granting agencies, newsletters, and a computerized search system. It will be staffed by a highly skilled grants coordinator, who will assist area grant seekers to locate funding sources and prepare quality proposals. The coordinator will also serve as an advocate for local programs, visiting funding sources and attending conferences at which funding officials meet.

In short, the Area-Wide Grants Coordinating Office will give local organizations the tools they need to increase their levels of support. The office will give support in three main areas:

- *information*—on funding sources gathered and maintained in an extensive library

- *training*—given by the grants coordinator through seminars, state-of-the-art videotape series, etc.

- *advocacy*—the grants coordinator will maintain contact with grant makers, locate funding opportunities for local agencies, and help these agencies develop and present their ideas to funders

The Area-Wide Grants Coordinating Office will serve as a meeting place for local nonprofit agencies. It will be a place where they can discuss their work and initiate cooperative projects that make the most effective use of their resources.

Goals of the Area-Wide Grants Coordinating Office

1. Increase the number and quality of proposals submitted for funding by nonprofit organizations.
2. Improve the acceptance rate of the proposals submitted.
3. Encourage coordination between local nonprofit organizations. This is to include the sharing of information on funding sources and the creation of consortia projects pooling the resources of two or more local groups.
4. Help local organizations save time, money, and energy by teaching them to focus on only the most appropriate funding sources for their projects.
5. Serve as a center where local agencies, with the help of trained staff, can learn to improve their grant-seeking skills, find information on funding sources, and write more effective grant proposals.

First-Year Objectives of the Area-Wide Grants Coordinating Office

1. Sponsor and submit one hundred grant proposals during the first year of operation.
2. Enlist at least fifty organizations as charter members of the office. Members will be charged a nominal fee based on their use of office resources (depends on funder's wishes).
3. Form a comprehensive grants library for the use of grant seekers.
4. Have the capacity to become 50 percent self-sufficient through membership/user fees after the first year. The remaining 50 percent will come from grant support and fund-raising methods.
5. To publish twelve monthly newsletters on subjects related to grantsmanship, alert local organizations to funding opportunities, and keep member/users informed of the local funding picture.
6. To create a complete filing system, including information on funding sources as well as member experience with those funders. Files will be open to all member/users of the coordinating office. This will facilitate the sharing of experiences and the improvement of approaches to funding sources. The filing system will be in place and working after the first month of operation.

What the Area-Wide Grants Coordinating Office Will Do

The Area-Wide Grants Coordinating Office will be staffed by a grants coordinator and a full-time secretary. They will set up the office with the help of a consultant with expertise in the grants area. Once the office is set up, the coordinator and secretary will share responsibility for the following:

1. Organize and run a grants library.
2. Work with applicants to turn ideas into fundable proposals.
3. Review grants to avoid duplication of effort.
4. Serve as a resource to anyone with questions about grant funding.
5. Alert organizations in the community about funding opportunities.
6. Develop a skills bank of people who can be resources to grant applicants, then operate a referral service that matches resource people with appropriate applicants.
7. Provide planning tools and other instructional aids to grant applicants.
8. Maintain extensive research files on funding sources that make grants in the community, including basic data, lists of grants, guidelines, and records of other organizations' experiences in developing support.
9. Provide a community forum for funding-source representatives to inform grant applicants about the current funding scene.
10. Maintain a grants telephone hotline to answer immediate questions about funding regulations and deadlines.
11. Collect sample proposals, both successful and unsuccessful, to serve as guides for future grant applicants.
12. Maintain an extensive research system for the purpose of "webbing" the interconnections between and affiliations of various funding officials.
13. Provide standard forms for grant applicants to use that incorporate the key elements of successful approaches to funding sources (e.g., feasibility forms, research forms, evaluation forms.
14. Buy reports from professional research firms that are of interest to local organizations. These reports would normally be too expensive for just one organization.
15. Produce and distribute a confidential newsletter for members only about successes and failures with funding sources, including practical how-to information. Newsletter will also keep users of the office up-to-date on status of proposals submitted and grants received.
16. Help form special-interest committees to stimulate grants in specific subject areas and to help with specific grant programs. Typical committees could be in research, health, culture, education, youth projects, and so on.
17. Start a Grants Commission. Members would help in researching specific funding sources, introducing applicants to personal contacts, and informing applicants about current trends in government funding and legislation.
18. Maintain contact with funding sources through correspondence, telephone, and personal visits (state, regional, and national funders).
19. Act as a funding catalyst, suggesting new ideas for proposals, especially with regard to new and developing programs.
20. Provide consultation to applicants on proposal writing and grant-application procedures.
21. Review preliminary drafts of proposals for clarity and adherence to guidelines.
22. Assist applicants in preparation of budgets and final drafts.
23. Expedite and follow up on proposals after submission.

24. Monitor progress of grant after award, including verifying grant payments.

25. Assist in preparation of interim and final project reports and evaluations.

Evaluation

The success of the Area-Wide Grants Coordinating Office will be measured in two ways. First, we will compare our status at the end of year one with our stated objectives.

We also plan to conduct a survey of the members/users of the office. This survey will ask specific questions in the following three areas:

- how effective grant applications are now as compared with before the existence of the grants coordinating office

- how valuable the assistance of the grants coordinator was in grants solicitation activities

- how valuable the resources were at the office and which ones were most helpful

We will tally the survey results and then prepare a final report on the first-year results of the grants coordinating office based on both aspects of the evaluation. This report will also include statistical analysis of the success rate of the proposals submitted for funding through the Area-Wide Grants Coordinating Office.

Future Funding

This proposal is a request for the first two years of funding for the Area-Wide Grants Coordinating Office. After the first year, operation of the office should be much less expensive, as the following startup costs will have been paid:

- basic library expenses (not including ongoing costs like journal subscriptions and research-updating services),

- the costs associated with a consultant to assist in setting up a library and a filing and office system

- the purchase of office equipment

After year one of the program, we plan to develop support from the following three sources:

- 50 percent membership/user fees,

- 35–45 percent government, corporate, and foundation grants

- 5–15 percent fund-raising methods such as major gift and mail solicitation

Budget	Year 1	Year 2
Yearly Costs		
Grants Coordinator Salary	$25,000	$27,500
Office Manager/Secretary Salary	10,000	12,000
Employee Benefits	3,400	3,800
Library	10,000	4,000
Office Rent	2,400	2,400
Telephone (Regular & Hotline)	6,000	6,000
Printing	5,000	5,000
Newsletter	6,000	6,000
Bulletins	6,000	6,000
Travel (New York City and Other Locations)	5,000	5,000
Memberships in Professional Associations	1,000	1,000
Conference and Seminar Attendance	3,000	3,000
Start-Up Costs		
Consultant	4,000	1,000
TOTAL	$86,800	$82,700

Note: User fees should provide approximately 50 percent of the total budget during the second year. The more frequent the usage, the higher the fee.

GRANTS OFFICE INVENTORY

Chapter 5

Evaluating and Improving Your Grant Opportunity Research System

For Each Activity/Item Listed, Check Status:

Activity/Item	Reviewed, Appropriate Part of Grants Office	Reviewed, Appropriate Part of Other Office (List)	Reviewed, Not Applicable	Reviewed, Inappropriate Needs Action	Non-existent, Needs Action
1. Grants Information dissemination system A. Tailored Funding Research • funding source news-letters • computerized grants interest profiles B. Grants resource library					

Complete this Section for Each Activity/Item Needing Action:

What Needs to Be Accomplished? (Activity/Item)	By Whom? (Office/Person)	By When? (Time Frame)	Resources, Required— Personnel, Supplies, Equipment, Programming, etc.	Estimated Costs

GRANTS OFFICE INVENTORY

Chapter 5 *(continued)*

Evaluating and Improving Your Grant Opportunity Research System

For Each Activity/Item Listed, Check Status:

Activity/Item	Reviewed, Appropriate Part of Grants Office	Reviewed, Appropriate Part of Other Office (List)	Reviewed, Not Applicable	Reviewed, Inappropriate Needs Action	Non-existent, Needs Action
• books, journals, newsletters, govt. publications, magazines, etc. • computerized data-bases, information retrieval systems C. Community grants office/library or area-wide coordinating office					

Complete this Section for Each Activity/Item Needing Action:

What Needs to Be Accomplished? (Activity/Item)	By Whom? (Office/Person)	By When? (Time Frame)	Resources, Required— Personnel, Supplies, Equipment, Programming, etc.	Estimated Costs

CHAPTER 6

The Role of the Grants Office in Contacting Funding Sources

The grants office provides prospective grant seekers with varying degrees of assistance in the grants process. The grants-office administrator functions as a helper/administrator much like a traffic policeman who keeps people safe and things moving.

The job is a difficult one because the administrator often finds him or herself in conflicting roles. While the administrator should motivate and assist the grant writer, he or she must also continually maintain an awareness of the organization's mission. He or she must act as an administrator with responsibilities to the organization's mission, while considering his or her own personal grant interests and those of the organization's prospective grant seekers. And, above all, the grants-office administrator must report to a senior administrator who has his or her own grants agenda.

Although the job is difficult, it can be done. Maintaining a balance between all of the differing interests is possible when the organization has a grants-office mission statement that sets priorities for the grants effort and outlines a plan to accomplish these priorities. In the absence of such a statement, which is understood by all staff, the grants administrator is forced into an imbalance in the win-win formula and may side with the administration (the power and authority) at the expense of the staff (the idea generators). The mission of the organization is thus compromised, and everyone is a potential loser. To keep this from occurring, one must remember that all parties can win—and not at the expense of one faction over another.

Developing a Webbing and Linkage System for Private and Public Funding Sources

One important function that your grants office may provide is recording and monitoring the names of the friends of your organization who know specific funding officials, trustees, and/or board members. Since who you know may be more important than what you know or how you write a proposal, the organization that has a system to record and retrieve linkages operates from a significant advantage.

A friend of the organization with a link to a potential funding source can:

- help you discover the hidden agenda of the funding source

- arrange an opportunity for you to meet with the funding source

- attend such a meeting with you

There is no substitute for a well-designed project submitted by a credible organization to an appropriate funder. When you also have an advocate for your organization who the funder already knows and trusts, you have the best possible chances for success.

Who are these linkages? Where do you find them? Some links to funders may already be part of your organization. With a little cultivation and the building of trust, they will come forward.

The first step is teaching the staff, volunteers, board members, and advocates that the organization's ability to attract grant funds depends directly on its ability to communicate with the funder. Let them know that there is a 300 to 500 percent increase in success through preproposal contact with funders. Make sure they are aware of the role that the friends of your organization can play in such contact. Ask people to think about who they know, who their spouses know, and who their close friends know. Use a newsletter, meetings, and so on to get your point across.

Before you ask the friends of your organization to reveal their linkages, they should know how the information they provide will be used. The following are the rules that I consider basic to a good webbing and linkage system.

1. Let the friends of your organization know that the information they provide will be kept secure and that only a few people will have access to it. Give them the names of the people who will have access to the linkage data.
2. Assure them that they will be contacted to discuss their endorsement of the project *before* their name is used with any funding source. Let them know that they will be given the opportunity to approve or disapprove the plans to contact the funding source. (See the Webbing and Linkage Sample Cover Letter.) You will use them to contact their linkage to get your "foot-in-the-door."

How should you request linkage information? One way to begin building the base of contacts is to hand out a worksheet with a list of those funding sources that you are currently considering pursuing for grant funds (Webbing and Linkage Worksheet 1). Have your friends review the list for possible linkages. For government prospects, list program officers, directors, and even past grantees or reviewers that your research has uncovered. For foundation and corporate sources, list funding-source staff, the board members or trustees, and director. You may also want to add space or a separate worksheet for funding-source contacts other than those listed.

Another way to gather this linkage data is to distribute a questionnaire that requests the desired information but does not provide a list of funding sources (Webbing and Linkage Worksheet 2). While this approach is initially less time-consuming for you, my experience has shown that the return of useful information is much greater when there are specifics on the webbing and linkage worksheet. Also, it is easy to omit a linkage when the worksheet is open-ended. One advocate I worked with thought he would be embarrased if I saw him playing golf with a potential contact whose name he had not given. He much preferred a ready-made list containing funding-source names.

The best response to requests for linkage information occurs when the board demonstrates its support for the project by forming a special committee to gather this data. One organization I belong to has a linkage committee headed by a few of the board members: the vice-president of a major bank (from the trust department), a corporate board member, and a foundation trustee. These people have the respect of the other board members, the staff, the volunteers,

WEBBING AND LINKAGE
SAMPLE COVER LETTER

Date

Name
Title
Address

Dear _____ :

Our proposal-development effort has developed several approaches to meeting the need(s) of _____ .

Our success in receiving a grant to fund a proposal in this area is greatly enhanced when we can contact the funder before we write the proposal.

Please review the attached list of proposed funding sources and designate those that you may have a linkage to. (Or please list any funding sources that you have a linkage to.) The linkage may be through you directly or indirectly through a relative, acquaintance, or corporate/business affiliation.

You will always be approached by us for your approval and assistance in contacting the funding source *before* contact is actually made. Your responses will be strictly confidential and access of this information will be limited to _____ .

Your sharing of this information may be worth thousands of dollars in grants. It may also save hundreds of hours of volunteer and staff time spent in preparing proposals for the wrong funders.

Sincerely,

Name
Title
Phone Number

WEBBING AND LINKAGE WORKSHEET 1

Foundation

Name _____   *Board Members/Trustees*
Address _____   _____
Director _____   _____
Contact Person _____   _____
Notes _____
_____

Corporation

Name _____   *Corporate Board Members*
Address _____   _____
Contributions Officer _____   _____
_____   _____
Notes _____
_____

Government Agency

Agency _____   *Staff Members*
Address _____   _____
Program Officer _____   _____
Contact Person _____   _____
Notes _____
_____

Other Funding Source Contacts

_____
_____

WEBBING AND LINKAGE WORKSHEET 2

Your Name:

Address:

Phone Number:

---

1. What foundation or corporate boards are you or your spouse on?

2. Do you know anyone who is on a foundation or corporation board?
If so, please list.

3. Does your spouse know anyone on a foundation or corporation board?
If so, please list.

4. Have you served on any government committees?
If so, please list.

5. Do you know any government funding contacts?
If so, please list.

6. Please list the fraternal groups, social clubs, and/or service organizations that you are involved in.

You may also ask questions on educational background, military service, religious affiliation, political preference, job title and description, and ability to travel for business. Please note, however, that it is optional to ask for personal data.

and the advocates, and their requests for information result in responses.

After developing an effective strategy for collecting webbing and linkage data, your organization must be able to use this information to its fullest. In the days before microprocessors and personal computers, this data was kept on index cards. Even if you don't have computer equipment and data-entry staff, your linkage system may be the way to enter the electronic age.

At the first meeting of our webbing and linkage committee, the banker turned to the foundation trustee and said, "Will your foundation grant our organization $10,000 to get started on a linkage system?" Her answer was yes. In fact, she verbally granted us the money without even having a letter proposal, although we now need to submit a Letter Proposal for Initiating a Webbing and Linkage System for her files. The initiation of a linkage system was funded because key individuals perceived the usefulness and impact such a system could have on our grant seeking. Since these key individuals have "bought in" to the project monetarily and conceptually, they will be motivated to convince others to contribute to the linkages data base.

This particular group has decided to embark on a multiphase program to build its linkage base. The foundation area will addressed in the first phase, and the webbing and linkage program will stress "getting our foot in the door" of these private funding sources. Separate questionnaires aimed at uncovering linkages have been developed for board members, advisory committee members, staff, and volunteers.

The second phase will involve corporate linkages; state and federal contacts will be researched in phase three. Two types of linkages will be examined in phase three—elected officials, to assist in grant appropriation and contact with funding sources, and bureaucrats, especially those related to government grant programs.

If you already have the necessary computer equipment, a linkage system can provide the funds for added capacity, new programs, and equipment. By giving your organization the ability to effectively use the linkage information, a donor may take some credit for the grant monies the system generates.

Your grants linkage system will gain acceptance quickly and easily as long as it is kept separate from fund-raising. In the grant marketplace, the money *must* be given away, and in most cases, the money disseminated in a grant does not come from an *individual*. In fundraising you are asking an individual for his or her own money. Do

LETTER PROPOSAL FOR INITIATING A WEBBING AND LINKAGE SYSTEM

Date

Foundation Name:
Foundation Address:

Dear _____ :

We at _____ are grateful for your past support. In fact, your grant of $ _____ in 19 ___ has accomplished _____
_____ .
Your continued support of the area of _____ accounted for _____ % of your past year's grant. It is with our knowledge of your commitment to the area of _____ , and your interest and support of our organization, that I approach you with this proposal. (Start with a statement reflecting the giving pattern of the foundation as it relates to your organization and the need you must to reduce.)

Our area is fortunate to have _____ foundations and _____ major corporations that consistently demonstrate their philanthropic support of local nonprofits. This support has resulted in the growth and maturation of our organization. To sustain our development, we are now seeking to secure grant funds from the larger base of regional and national corporate and private foundations.

Although we have the projects and ability to prepare outstanding proposals that could draw grant monies into our local area, we lack a track record and familiarity with these foundations. What we are missing is a system to determine individuals who could help us contact these funding sources. A study in *Grants Magazine* reported that organizations that contacted funding sources *before* they wrote proposals experienced a 500 percent increase in grant-proposal acceptance. As you can see, knowing "who you know" could be worth its weight in gold (grants).

We invite the _____ Foundation to invest with us in the development of a computerized webbing and linkage system. First, we will survey the volunteers, board members, advocates, and friends of our organization to ascertain who they know on major corporate and foundation boards and/or staffs. The results of this survey will then be entered into a personal computer retrieval system. Individuals and their linkages will be held in the strictest confidence, and no one from our staff will contact a funder without prior approval from the individual supplying the linkage. In some instances, an individual will be invited to accompany a member of our organization on a personal visit to the funding source.

Last year foundations granted over _____ billion dollars, and corporate grants totaled _____ billion. We know that part of this _____ billion dollars could be granted to our area of _____ . This project seeks to discover how much of these funds might be granted to us and who could assist us in this endeavor.

We are uniquely suited to put a system of linkages to use. We have a distinguished and motivated board, staff, and volunteer base.

We are requesting $ _____ from the _____ Foundation. These funds will be used for the following:

Personal Computer	$ _____
Laser Printer	$ _____
Software	$ _____
Data Entry	$ _____
TOTAL	$ _____

You can be confident that your investment will provide a return worthy of your support and will truly be a gift that keeps on giving.

Sincerely,

Name
Title
Phone Number

not mix your grants-linkage system with fund-raising or you will find
that your linkages are severely reduced.

The grants linkage system can be organized around a particular
area, program, or part of your organization, or it can be organized
around your entire organization. Since individuals have a tendency
to relate to problems, or particular programs or solutions, it may be
easiest to capitalize on these focused interests in building support for
your linkage system.

The individual with the appropriate linkage may assist you in
contacting a certain funding source, or go with you or your project
director to see the funding source. Be aware, however, that when
your linkages become involved in endorsing a project or proposal,
they may take liberty in negotiating the grant amount or changing
the project to fit the funder without checking with the grants administrator or project director. While involvement and endorsement
is encouraged, the *need* is what the linkage is endorsing. The program
or project design is the purview of the experts and program initiator.

Another problem that surfaces when a linkage system is developed
is that you may be tempted to write a proposal to a funder that you
discovered a linkage to even though the proposal is not a priority.
In fact, it may not even move your organization toward meeting its
mission. Be careful of this. Remember, the reason for the linkage
system is to locate linkages to funders that you have identified as
interested in your proposals. If you have a strong linkage to a
funding source that is clearly inappropriate for your proposal/project,
explain the need for the project to the funder, mention that you
know the project is not a priority of the funder's, and ask if they
know of an appropriate funding source and could assist you in
contacting them. This could result in a positive relationship with the
initial funding source and improve your organization's image, since
the source will know your organization does its grants homework.

Contacting and Monitoring Public Funding Sources

The use of the grants office as the control center for monitoring
contact with funding sources is vital to maintaining a positive image
of the organization in the grants' marketplace. No one should be
allowed to carry the name of the organization or imply organizational
knowledge and consent for contact and ideas unless he or she is
designated to hold that authority.

Many well-intentioned grant seekers have misrepresented their
organizations by:

- taking inferior-quality proposals to funders

- requesting inappropriate grant amounts

- submitting a proposal to a funding source without knowing if other proposals from their organization have recently been submitted to the same source

- visiting a funding source to discuss a proposal and meeting another grant seeker from their own organization in the reception area

In order to demonstrate to a funder that you will be able to attend to the details of administering a proposal after it is awarded, it is important to show adequate administration of the preproposal phases of grant seeking. To maintain a high-quality image of your organization, evaluate your preproposal-contact controls and procedures, and determine the role and function of your grants office in this area.

The importance of preproposal contact with government funding sources cannot be overemphasized. In a study of ten thousand federal proposals, the only significant variable separating the funded and rejected proposals was preproposal contact with the funding source. Chances for success go up from 300 to 500 percent when contact is made with the funding source *before* the proposal is written. Remember, you must not write the proposal until you are knowledgeable about the funding source. Having information on the funding source, such as past grantees, reviewers, and so on, will pay off because you will be viewed as a knowledgeable partner in the grants process.

Contact by letter, phone, and when possible, a personal visit should be encouraged. One way to encourage yourself to follow a systematic method of approaching funding sources is to set up a schedule of preproposal contact. For example:

Week 1: Write to two funding sources.
Week 2: Write to two more funding sources.
Week 3: Call the two funding sources you wrote to in Week 1 and ask for an appointment.
Week 4: Call the two funding sources you wrote to in Week 2 and ask for an appointment.
Week 5: Follow up on appointments from phone conversations.

In some organizations and institutions, contacting prospective funders is the sole purview of the grants office; in others, individual grant seekers are encouraged to initiate preprosal contact. In either case, the following letters and worksheets offer guidance on how to address this important aspect of grant seeking.

The Sample Letter to a Federal Agency for Mailing List and Past Grantees, Sample Letter to a Federal Agency for a List of Reviewers, and Sample Letter to Federal Agency for an Appointment have been designed to assist you in organizing your preproposal-contact effort and to help you develop a procedures manual for this area. For your convenience, they have been incorporated into a software package entitled GRANTWINNER, available for purchase through David G. Bauer Associates, Inc.

USING THE PHONE WITH PUBLIC FUNDING SOURCES

Calling federal and state funding sources can be very frustrating. Often the contact name or telephone number derived from preliminary research is incorrect. If your information proves inaccurate, question the individual you do reach. Ask who the actual contact person is and how to reach him or her. Also, your grants office can help by enlisting the services of the individual in your congressperson's office designated to assist people in your district with grants.

Naturally, the best preproposal-contact approach is to see the funding source in person. If you cannot do so, however, try to gather the same information over the phone that you would face to face. Although it is harder to "read" what the funding source is saying over the phone than on a personal visit, you want the same results. Your goal is to increase your chances of success by finding out how to meet the needs of the funding source. Review the suggestions found in this chapter under the section entitled Questions to Ask a Program Officer.

MAKING AN APPOINTMENT WITH A PUBLIC FUNDING SOURCE

Objective: To obtain an interview with the highest-ranking person in the program.

Step 1: Call and ask for the program officer. If the program officer is not available, proceed to Step 2.

Step 2: Get the program officer's secretary's name and ask when his or her boss can be reached.

Step 3: Call back. Try person-to-person. Alternative plans would be to ask an advocate to set up the appointment, to get congressional

SAMPLE LETTER TO A FEDERAL AGENCY
FOR
MAILING LIST AND PAST GRANTEES

Date

Name
Title
Address

Dear _____ :

Our organization is developing a project that we would like to have funded under your program _____ .

Please add me to your mailing list to receive the necessary application forms, program guidelines, and any other information you feel would be helpful to me in this endeavor. A list of last year's grant recipients under this program would be very much appreciated.

I have enclosed a self-addressed stamped envelope for your convenience in returning the list of successful grantees. Thank you for your cooperation and assistance in this matter.

Sincerely,

Name
Title
Phone Number

SAMPLE LETTER TO A FEDERAL AGENCY
FOR
A LIST OF REVIEWERS

Date

Name
Title
Address

Dear _____ :

I am at present developing a proposal for funds administered by your office. I would find it very helpful to have a list of last year's reviewers. Such a list would assist me in developing my approach and the appropriate writing style. Please advise me if the makeup or background of the review committee will change significantly in the next funding cycle for program _____ .

My proposal is based upon the level, expertise, and diversity of the reviewers. Information on the composition of the review committee will be used to prepare a quality proposal based upon the reviewers' backgrounds.

I have enclosed a self-addressed stamped envelope for your convenience in responding to this request. I appreciate your effort to provide me with this information.

Sincerely,

Name
Title
Phone Number

SAMPLE LETTER TO A FEDERAL AGENCY FOR AN APPOINTMENT

Date

Name
Title
Address

Dear _____ :

My research on your funding program indicates that a project we have developed would be appropriate for consideration by your agency for funding under _____ .

I would appreciate five to ten minutes of your time to discuss my project. Your insights, knowledge, and information on any grants that have been funded using a similar approach would be invaluable. My travel plans call for me to be in your area on _____ .

I will phone to confirm the possibility of a brief meeting to discuss this important proposal.

Sincerely,

Name
Title
Phone Number

help in making the appointment, and/or to try going in cold early in the week to get an appointment for later in the week. (They may prefer to see you then to get you out of the way.)

Step 4: If all of the above steps fail, ask the secretary who else can answer technical questions concerning the program. You may get an appointment with a screen, but it will be better than talking to yourself!

Step 5: When you finally get a program person on the phone, introduce yourself and give a *brief* description of your organization and project, research, and so on. Let the program person know that the need for your project or research is extreme, that your organization is uniquely suited to conduct the research or project, and that you understand that the funding source's program deals with these needs. Tell him or her that you would like an appointment to discuss the program and your approaches. Be sure to mention that you are planning a trip in the vicinity and that you have a flexible schedule.

When you get an appointment, stop talking and hang up. If no appointment is possible, say that you have some questions that you can ask over the phone and request five minutes of his or her time now or later. Ask the same questions you would ask in person see (Questions to Ask Program Officer).

THE VISIT: FACE-TO-FACE CONTACT WITH A PUBLIC FUNDING SOURCE

The object of face-to-face contact with a representative of a funding source is to discover as much as possible about the source and how they award their grants. With this information, you can produce a proposal that reflects a sensitivity to their needs. Before you make a visit, review your Funding-Source Staff Profile, and after you make contact, fill in the Public Funding Source Contact Summary Sheet.

The image you create through your personal contact can place your organization in a positive position for years. You want the funder to love you, to be your advocate with reviewers, and to do so, you must look and talk like the funder thinks you should. Remember, the more you differ from what the funder expects and desires, the greater the problems with communication and agreement. Dress is a critical factor in establishing your credibility. If you do not know the source's expectations on dress, play it safe and read *Dress for Success* by John T. Molloy. (Molloy's initial research on dress was carried out under a grant.)

QUESTIONS TO ASK A PROGRAM OFFICER

- Do you agree that our project addresses an important need?

- What do you expect to be the average size of your grant awards this year?

- How will successful grantees from last year affect people submitting new or first applications? Will last year's grantees be in competition with me, or have their funds been set aside? If so, how much is left for new awards?

- Are there any unannounced programs or unsolicited proposals available to fund an important project like ours?

- What is the most common mistake or flaw in proposals submitted to you?

- Are there any areas you would like to see addressed in a proposal that may have been overlooked by the other grantees or applicants?

- We have discussed several approaches to this needs area. You may know whether any of these have been tried. Could you review our approaches and provide us with any guidance?

- Do you review or critique proposals if they are developed early?

- Would you recommend a previously funded proposal for us to read for format and style? (Remember, you are entitled to read *any* funded proposal, but don't be too pushy.)

- Is your program geared toward a specific type of grant (e.g., consultant, demonstration, evaluation)?

- The guidelines call for _____ copies of the proposal. Could you use more? May I bind the copies in inexpensive binders?

- Are there any problems created by my use of tabs to separate the different sections of the proposal?

FUNDING-SOURCE STAFF PROFILE

Before each visit to a funding source, review this sheet to be sure you are bringing the correct materials, advocates, and staff.

Funding source _____
Agency director _____
Program director _____
Contact person _____ Title _____

Profile

Name _____
Date of birth _____ Place of birth _____
Education: college _____
          postgraduate _____
Work experience _____
_____
_____
_____

Military service _____
Service clubs _____
_____

Religious affiliation _____
Interests/hobbies _____
_____

Publications _____
_____
_____

Comments _____
_____
_____
_____
_____
_____

PUBLIC FUNDING SOURCE CONTACT SUMMARY SHEET

Add to this sheet each time you contact a public funding source.

Project title _____
_____

Agency name _____
Program officer _____
Contacted on (date) _____
Contacted by whom _____
Contacted by: Letter _____ Phone _____ Personal contact _____
Staff and/or advocates present _____
_____

Discussed _____
_____
_____
_____
_____
_____
_____

Results _____
_____
_____
_____
_____
_____
_____

To ensure that it presents a proper image, your organization should review its guidelines for dress and other aspects of personal contact with funders. You may wish to incorporate the following suggestions in your guidelines for contacting funding sources.

1. Have two people visit the funding source. Consider sending an advocate or graduate of your program rather than a paid staff member. Try to match age, interests, education, and so on with those of the funding executive whenever possible.
2. Bring materials that help demonstrate the need in the specific field of interest. Bring your Proposal-Development Workbook as well as audiovisual aids, such as short film strips or videotapes that focus on the need for the project or research, rather than on your organization. (Be sure that you can operate the audiovisual equipment with ease. Bring extension cords, adapters, replacement bulbs, and so on.)
3. Role-play with your team member. Know who will take responsibility for the different parts or segments of your presentation.
4. Have information on your proposal, but *never* leave a proposal with the funding executive. Preproposal contact is based on the premise that you are there to gather information that you will use in your proposal preparation. By leaving a proposal, you are demonstrating that you had no intention of using the time that he or she invested in you to improve your proposal.

COORDINATING CONTACT WITH PAST GRANTEES AND REVIEWERS

Your grants office may coordinate contacts with past grantees and reviewers. The information gathered from these individuals can be invaluable in assisting you in your approach to the funding source. The following suggested questions for past grantees and reviewers should be helpful to you and may be placed in your grants-office procedures manual.

QUESTIONS FOR PAST GRANTEES

You have requested a list of previous grantees by letter and enclosed a self-addressed stamped envelope for the funding source's convenience. You may have also requested the list again by phone. If necessary, let the funding source know that you are entitled to know who received funding under the Sunshine Law or Freedom of

Information Act. You may also ask your congressperson to obtain the list for you.

Once you have the list, select a grantee that is not in proximity to you. Call the grantee and tell them where you got his or her name. Ask to speak to the director or person who worked on the proposal. In general, past grantees will feel flattered that you called. Ask questions from the following list.

- Did you call or go to see the funding source before writing the proposal?

- Who on the funding source's staff did you find most helpful?

- How did you use your advocates or congresspeople?

- Did you have the funding source review or critique your proposal before its final submission?

- Did you use consultants to help you on the proposal?

- Was there a hidden agenda to the Request for Proposal (RFP)?

- When did you begin the process of developing your application and contacting the funding source?

- What materials did you find the most helpful in developing your proposal?

- Did the funding source come to see you for a site visit before the proposal was awarded? After it was awarded? Who came? What did this representative wear? How old was he or she? Would you characterize him or her as conservative, moderate, or liberal? Did anything in the process surprise you?

- How close was your initial budget to the awarded amount? (You can verify this information by looking at the grantee's proposal when you visit the funding source.)

- Who negotiated the budget?

- What would you do differently next time?

QUESTIONS FOR PAST REVIEWERS

You have requested a list of reviewers. Again, by the Sunshine Law, you can demand one, but don't. Tell the funding source you are concerned about the makeup or background of the reviewers. If they are reluctant to give names, try to get general information on the reviewers and the process. Unfortunately, the federal government frowns on contact with past reviewers. However, just remember that discussions with past reviewers can be very beneficial.

You may start your conversation by identifying yourself and telling the individual that you understand he or she was a reviewer for the program. Then proceed with the following questions.

- How did you get to be a reviewer?
- Did you review proposals at the funding source's location or at your home?
- What training or instructions did the funding source give you?
- Did you follow a point system? If so, please describe it.
- What were you told to look for?
- How would you write a proposal differently now that you have been a reviewer?
- What were the most common mistakes that you saw?
- Did you meet other reviewers?
- How many proposals were you given to read?
- How much time did you have to read them?
- How did the funding source handle discrepancies in point assignments?
- What did the representative of the funding source wear, say, and do during the review process?
- Did you know about a staff review to follow your review?

Contacting and Monitoring Private Funding Sources

As with government funding sources, contact with private funding sources before you write proposals is crucial to a successful proposal. Preproposal contact enables you to gather information concerning the funding source, including their needs and particular approaches or methods they find interesting. You can use this information to tailor your proposal specifically to the funding source.

However, since many private funding sources are short on staff, it may be difficult to arrange contact with them. Often you will find that addresses for these sources are actually those of trust departments of banks. Your best bet for establishing contact may be using your webbing and linkage connections to secure a visit with a trustee or board member. *The Foundation Directory* is cross-referenced by names of board members to aid you in the process of determining who knows whom.

Although difficult to achieve, personal contact with private funding sources is possible if you arrange it in an organized, strategic manner. The process should consist of writing a letter, making a telephone call, and visiting the funding source.

THE INQUIRY LETTER

Requesting basic information on a funding source through correspondence is desirable. The results of this request will enable you to gather valuable information on the funding source. Therefore, this letter should always be sent before you write to the funding executive for an appointment. The Sample Letter to a Private Funding Source for Basic Information (Inquiry Letter) illustrates how to word correspondence of this type.

THE APPOINTMENT LETTER

It's always a good idea to arrange an initial interview with a funding source before you submit a proposal. The best ways to set up such a meeting are by letter and telephone. The Sample Letter to a Private Funding Source for an Appointment will help you develop your own request for an appointment. Please note, however, that the information you obtained from sending your initial inquiry letter may indicate that an appointment letter is not what the funding source desires. The funding source may prefer a one- to two-page letter proposal summarizing your request.

TELEPHONING A PRIVATE FUNDING SOURCE FOR AN APPOINTMENT

Your chances of having the right phone number for a private funding source are much greater than for a public one. But what do you say when you make the call?

- Ask for the funding official by name if possible.

SAMPLE LETTER TO A
PRIVATE FUNDING SOURCE
FOR BASIC INFORMATION
(INQUIRY LETTER)

Date

Name
Title
Address

Dear _____ :

We have developed a project that benefits _____ .

Your support of this project would constitute a significant contribution in this field, which we understand is one of the important concerns of

_____ .

We would appreciate receiving information on your desired format for proposals, current priority statements, and other guidelines. Please add us to your mailing list for annual reports, newsletters, and other material you think might be useful to us as we work on this and related projects.

I will be calling you in the near future to discuss our opportunities to work together. Thank you for your cooperation.

Sincerely,

Name
Title
Phone Number

SAMPLE LETTER TO A PRIVATE FUNDING SOURCE FOR AN APPOINTMENT

Date

Name
Title
Address

Dear _____ :

I am interested in meeting with you to discuss an important project that deals with _____ .

In researching this field, I have noticed serious, active interest on the part of _____ .

Since we are analyzing several possible approaches, your input at this time would be most valuable in our formal proposal development. A few minutes of your time would enable us to more closely meet both your concerns and our interest in this field.

I will call you to arrange a brief meeting at your convenience.

Sincerely,

Name
Title
Phone Number

- Tell the official you will be in the area and would like to meet with him or her briefly to discuss a project that your research indicates the source would be interested in.

- Ask for an appointment.

If the funding official agrees to see you, make the necessary arrangements and hang up.

If the funding official will not grant you an appointment because the foundation or corporate policy does not allow visits by prospective grantees, arrange a phone interview for a later date (see the following section on telephone interviews), and/or ask if he or she has a travel schedule and would like to visit your site to see your program. If one of your advocates is going to be talking to a funding source board member, you should let the funding official know. He or she will probably be more willing to talk with you in order to be able to field questions from the board member.

If the official will not grant you an appointment because of a lack of interest in your project, ask why this is so. Unfortunately, it can take years for changes in the interests of funding sources to show up in resource tools. Also, ask who else might be interested in your project. Funding sources often know one another and have inside knowledge of who is funding what.

If you can't get through to a funding offical at all, use the intermediaries and ask them intelligent questions (see the worksheet entitled Questions to Ask a Funding Source at the First Meeting). In addition, make sure to let them know that you *will* call back. Most people try once and give up. You must be persistent.

THE TELEPHONE INTERVIEW

It is often difficult to get a funding official to give you time for an in-person meeting to discuss your project, or it may be inconvenient and/or expensive to set up such a meeting. While a face-to-face contact is the first choice, in those cases when it is not an option, conduct a phone interview with the funding official.

The following checklist details a four-step process to follow each time you discuss your project over the phone with a funding source. The data you would like to obtain or validate from the phone call include:

- the organization's current granting priorities

- specific information on how you should change your project and/or proposal to make it more attractive to the funding source

- proposal-format guidelines or, if there are no guidelines, information on the format preferred by the board members

- the most appropriate grant size to request

Keep in mind the following tips.

- Phone midweek.

- Use the funding executive's name.

- Mention who referred you to the funding source.

- Refer to any correspondence you have already sent to the funding source.

- Request five minutes. Let the official know you will call back if it is not convenient at that time.

THE VISIT: FACE-TO-FACE CONTACT WITH A PRIVATE FUNDING SOURCE

A face-to-face interview is the most personal and direct way of making contact with a funding-source executive. It is an invaluable tool in developing a relationship with that funding source. Your chances of making a good impression and of understanding the information you are given are much greater in person than on the phone.

One technique that you may want to try is the just-dropped-by-to-have-a-look visit. In this case, you will get the best reception by being sincerely interested in the general operation of the agency or organization and its giving program, goals, and activities. This is a field trip of sorts. Tell the funding official about your organization, share your interests and your future plans, and leave the funding official information on your overall organization. You do not need to discuss the project you hope will be funded, and you should not leave any information concerning the project.

A variation to this technique is to drop by Monday to arrange an appointment for whenever is convenient (later in the week, etc.). Most funding officials will realize that you are serious and that you will be coming back.

The other type of visit is the prearranged appointment. For this meeting, you have called or written ahead and have probably already shared some general introductory information.

Once you have arranged your appointment, consider the following questions (see also Questions to Ask a Funding Source at the First Meeting).

1. *Who is the best person(s) to represent us at the meeting?* Your representative at the first meeting should be an articulate committee member of your organization. He or she should also be a high-ranking member of your organization and a prime mover in the project you are trying to fund. One of the best approaches is to use an advocate from your advisory committee who is not and will not be paid by your organization or project. The time and concern of the unpaid advocate will give you instant credibility. No more than two people should be sent, or you will scare the funding source. The dress of the people sent is more important in private philanthropy than public (although it is important there also). Dress to create the image that your research suggests the funding source would like you to have. (By calling a past grantee, you may be able to find out the age and values of the funding official.)

2. *What materials should be brought to the meeting?* The materials needed are best collected and organized in your proposal-development workbook. You may want to bring additional materials to document the need for the project or research. Use simple audiovisual aides that are in balance with your proposed request. For example, a video presentation costing $10,000 would be an inappropriate accompaniment for a $5,000 grant request. Visuals should be used to demonstrate need and develop agreement on the importance of meeting this need. The funding source needs to know that you have developed several possible approaches to meeting this need and that you are there to learn which approach they are most interested in. Remember, you are not there to sell or convince them on one particular approach. Your idea summary sheet and cost benefit analysis worksheets will elicit more than enough response to begin a fruitful conversation. And most important, be ready to use parts of your proposal-development workbook to answer such questions as, "Why should we give the money to you instead of another organization in your field?"

QUESTIONS TO ASK A FUNDING SOURCE AT THE FIRST MEETING

Review these questions to determine which will be the most beneficial to ask based on your current knowledge of the funding source. If another individual is going with you to see the funding official, you may find it helpful to role-play with him or her using these questions.

1. Having reviewed last year's rules, will there be any changes? If so, what are they?

2. Last year the amount of funds awarded by your organization to our type of project was approximately _____ , and the average grant size was _____ . Will this remain consistent?

3. Our research indicates that your deadlines were _____ and _____ . Will they be the same this year?

4. Do proposals that are submitted early receive favorable treatment?

5. Who do you use to review proposals? Reviewers? Outside experts? Board members? Staff?

6. Are these your current granting priorities? (Give the funding official a copy of your research sheet.)

7. How do you look upon the submission of more than one proposal in a funding cycle?

8. Is this project idea eligible for funding under your guidelines?

9. Is our budget estimate realistic?

10. Would you look over my proposal if I finished it early?

11. Can you suggest other funding sources appropriate for this project?

12. May I see a proposal you have funded that was well liked for its style and/or format?

PRIVATE FUNDING SOURCE REPORT FORM

Each time a member of your staff contacts a funder in person or over the telephone, he or she should complete a Private Funding Source Report Form and put it in your files.

This simple procedure has a number of important benefits.

- You do not have to reinvent the wheel each time you speak with the funding source, or worry about damaging your image by discussing issues you have already discussed with the funder.

- You always have a source of current information on the funding source.

- You do not have to waste time locating people in your organization who have contacted the funder to ask them basic questions such as amount to request, name of person to whom you should submit the proposal, and proposal emphasis.

- You avoid the embarrassment of contradicting something said by a colleague in a previous contact with the funder.

This form should be reproduced and distributed to all advocates who may make contact with funders. Completed forms should be filed under the names of the funders and referred to before subsequent contacts with those funders.

Remember, one of your main objectives is to uncover the hidden agenda of the funding source and any information on priorities and how they may affect you.

COORDINATING CONTACT WITH ADVOCATES

Advocates can increase the credibility of the organization and provide valuable assistance to your funding effort. The development of an advocacy file will help you coordinate contact with your advocates. An advocacy file will provide for the one-stop location of:

- lists of advocates used by the organization

- lists of advisory committee members

- advocate endorsement letters

- a directory of interested individuals with various skills who will represent the organization on potential advisory committees, etc.

PRIVATE FUNDING SOURCE REPORT FORM

Complete this form after each contact with a private funding source.

Name of Funding Source _____

Address of Funding Source _____

Name of Person Spoken to at Funding Agency _____

Title of Person Spoken to _____

Phone Number and Extension of Person Spoken to _____

Date of Contact _____

Type of Contact: Phone _____   In Person _____

Name of Person Who Made Contact _____

Phone Number and Extension of Person Who Made Contact _____

Objective of Contact _____

_____

_____

_____

_____

_____

_____

_____

Results of Contact _____

_____

_____

_____

_____

_____

_____

_____

The lack of coordination in this important area can result in advocacy "burnout," created by:

- multiple requests to individual advocates for endorsement letters from several grant seekers

- repeated requests due to lost or misfiled letters

- the requesting of an advocate to become a member of an advisory committee when he or she is already on one or more

GRANTS OFFICE INVENTORY
Chapter 6
The Role of the Grants Office in Contacting Funding Sources

For Each Activity/Item Listed, Check Status:

Activity/Item	Reviewed, Appropriate Part of Grants Office	Reviewed, Appropriate Part of Other Office (List)	Reviewed, Not Applicable	Reviewed, Inappropriate Needs Action	Non-existent, Needs Action
1. Webbing and linkage system • record of "friends" of organization • method or system to ascertain links between friends and funders (questionnaires, etc.) • computerized system to record, store, up-date, maintain and					

Complete this Section for Each Activity/Item Needing Action:

What Needs to Be Accomplished? (Activity/Item)	By Whom? (Office/Person)	By When? (Time Frame)	Resources, Required—Personnel, Supplies, Equipment, Programming, etc.	Estimated Costs

GRANTS OFFICE INVENTORY

Chapter 6 *(continued)*

The Role of the Grants Office in Contacting Funding Sources

For Each Activity/Item Listed, Check Status:

Activity/Item	Reviewed, Appropriate Part of Grants Office	Reviewed, Appropriate Part of Other Office (List)	Reviewed, Not Applicable	Reviewed, Inappropriate Needs Action	Non-existent, Needs Action
retrieve linkage information • linkage committee with some board representation 2. Preproposal contact controls or a system-atic method for approaching funding sources					

Complete this Section for Each Activity/Item Needing Action:

What Needs to Be Accomplished? (Activity/Item)	By Whom? (Office/ Person)	By When? (Time Frame)	Resources, Required— Personnel, Supplies, Equipment, Programming, etc.	Estimated Costs

GRANTS OFFICE INVENTORY

Chapter 6 *(continued)*

The Role of the Grants Office in Contacting Funding Sources

For Each Activity/Item Listed, Check Status:

Activity/Item	Reviewed, Appropriate Part of Grants Office	Reviewed, Appropriate Part of Other Office (List)	Reviewed, Not Applicable	Reviewed, Inappropriate Needs Action	Non-existent, Needs Action
• standardized letters for: getting on mailing lists, requesting lists of reviewers, obtaining an appointment, getting basic information • sample lists of questions to ask: funding officers, past grantees, past reviewers					

Complete this Section for Each Activity/Item Needing Action:

What Needs to Be Accomplished? (Activity/Item)	By Whom? (Office/ Person)	By When? (Time Frame)	Resources, Required— Personnel, Supplies, Equipment, Programming, etc.	Estimated Costs

93

GRANTS OFFICE INVENTORY

Chapter 6 *(continued)*
The Role of the Grants Office in Contacting Funding Sources

For Each Activity/Item Listed, Check Status:

Activity/Item	Reviewed, Appropriate Part of Grants Office	Reviewed, Appropriate Part of Other Office (List)	Reviewed, Not Applicable	Reviewed, Inappropriate Needs Action	Non-existent, Needs Action
• standardized form for recording information on funding source staff (Profile Form) • standardized form for summarizing each contact made with a funding source • system for coordinating contact with advocates					

Complete this Section for Each Activity/Item Needing Action:

What Needs to Be Accomplished? (Activity/Item)	By Whom? (Office/ Person)	By When? (Time Frame)	Resources, Required— Personnel, Supplies, Equipment, Programming, etc.	Estimated Costs

CHAPTER 7

The Role of the Grants Office in Promoting an Organized Proposal

The grants office can have a dramatic effect on the perception that prospective grant seekers have of the grants process. Your office can make proposal preparation appear organized, controllable, and accomplishable.

Developing and distributing a grants-office procedure manual to all staff members will educate them about the role of your office. In addition to a description of how your organization processes grants, consider including a packet of helpful checklists and worksheets for distribution to each grant seeker. Ultimately, increased organizational skills and accurate expectations will make your job easier and assist the grant seeker in producing a better proposal.

Review the following worksheets, checklists, and grant tools and identify those items that you can use to assist the grant seeker with idea generation, grant writing, budget preparation, and so on. *The "How To" Grants Manual,* available through Macmillan Publishing Company, contains more detailed information on the areas mentioned in this chapter. Remember that the checklists and worksheets found throughout this chapter and book should be tailored to your organization, and not all of them need to be included in your manual.

Organizing Proposal Ideas for Marketing/Proposal Development Workbook

One function of the grants administrator's job is to help prospective grant seekers organize their proposal ideas. This assistance must be rendered in such a way that it:

- supports the monitoring and quality-control functions of the grants office

- provides the tools necessary for the marketing of proposals

- organizes the process, and thus saves time for the organization, the administration, and the proposal developer

Grant writers often find the application process complex and difficult since it is often expected to be accomplished during "spare time" or integrated into a demanding job description. Many grant writers become overwhelmed because they look at the big picture only—the completed proposal. As a result, they procrastinate and avoid approaching the application until the deadline is close and it is too late to do an adequate job.

The Swiss cheese concept, developed in Allan Lakein's book *How to Get Control of Your Time and Your Life,* is a time-management strategy that can help the grant seeker make the process of preparing and applying for grants more organized and less overwhelming. The proposal developer can be thought of as a mouse who must move a large piece of cheese. Rather than attempting to eat or move the cheese in one large piece, the mouse would eat holes in the cheese or move one little piece at a time. The grant seeker can take a similar approach: He or she must divide the grants process into pieces and tackle each piece individually until the task is completed. Taken one step at a time, the proposal-development process will not be overwhelming.

The steps necessary to organize and produce a grant application are logical and follow a definite order. By focusing on the steps or activities leading to the finished proposal, proposal preparation seems more accomplishable. The steps are listed below. The first ten assist the proposal developer in putting ideas in written form, developing reactions to these ideas, and evaluating the original idea and variation on that idea to produce the most fundable project.

1. developing and evaluating your project ideas
2. redefining your project ideas

3. documenting the need for your project
4. determining your organization's uniquenesses
5. developing your case statement
6. using advocates
7. organizing a project-advisory committee
8. choosing the correct funding-source marketplace
9. researching your chosen funding-source marketplace
10. contacting your prospective funding sources

The next eight steps assist the grant writer in developing his or her proposal.

11. developing your problem/needs statement
12. writing your objectives
13. developing your methods
14. developing your project planner
15. evaluation
16. future funding
17. dissemination
18. budget

The remaining ten steps assists the proposal developer in the significant tasks of writing and submitting the proposal.

19. Proposal Introduction
20. Title Page
21. Summary Abstract
22. Attachments
23. Cover Letter
24. Letter Proposal
25. Proposal-Review Committee
26. Submission: Private Source
27. Submission: Public Source
28. Outcome and Follow-up

Before tackling these steps, it is helpful to set up a proposal-development workbook or Swiss cheese book for each of the major areas of interest of the grant seeker.

A proposal-development workbook consists of a three-ring binder with a tab or divider for each of the steps outlined above. The proposal writer places information collected over time in the appropriate sections. This will reduce the time wasted frantically searching for information at the last minute. In addition, you can arrange to have standard information about your organization inserted into the proper sections (e.g., case statement). By placing helpful information in the workbooks in advance, you will enhance your image as an organized and efficient partner in the grant-seeking process and show your staff that you are sensitive to the time they invest in the grants process and value their efforts. I estimate that the use of the proposal-development workbook will save up to 50 percent of the time ordinarily spent in proposal preparation.

In addition, the proposal-organizing workbook provides the grant seeker with information to answer the funding official's questions during preproposal contact. Finally, when personal contact by the proposal developer is not possible, the grants administrator can do a more credible job representing the prospective grant seeker to funders by consulting the grant seeker's workbook.

The proposal-development workbook tabs are outlined in detail in *The "How To" Grants Manual* (Ace/Macmillan). A set of detailed tabs can be purchased from David G. Bauer Associates, Inc.

Needs Statement/Objectives/Methods

The following is a brief discussion of the needs statement and objectives and methods section of a proposal. The Grant-Writing Checklist and the Tailoring Worksheet that follow will assist the grant seeker in designing and writing his or her proposal. For more detailed information, see *The "How To" Grants Manual* (Macmillan Publishing).

NEEDS STATEMENT

Most grant seekers feel strongly about the need for their project. Too many assume that funding sources share their same feelings of concern and forget that the funding source has to choose between many interesting proposals. To increase your chances of funding, you must document the existence of a problem or need that is viewed by the funding source as a state of affairs that can be better, improved, or different.

Collect data that demonstrates need and keep it in your Proposal-Development Workbook. When you are ready to write a tailored proposal, select the items that you think will be the most convincing to your particular funding source.

GRANT-WRITING CHECKLIST

The proposal must be organized in the *exact* manner prescribed by the funder. Do not change the order requested.

The order that the proposal is submitted is rarely the order in which it is written. As you write each of the main sections of your proposal, make certain that you have addressed the following items.

Needs Statement/Search of Relevant Literature

_____ Statement is clear and concise

_____ Well-chosen, documented statistics

_____ Motivating and compelling—sense of urgency

_____ Objective with a variety of sources cited

_____ Documents gap between what is and what ought to be

_____ Documentation matched to reader/reviewer

Objectives

_____ Measurement indicators established

_____ Performance indicators established

_____ Time frame for completion established

_____ Cost estimate in objective

Methods/Activities

_____ Written clearly

_____ Sequence and relationship of activities clear

_____ Project personnel's time allocated by activities

_____ Time frames for activities outlined

TAILORING WORKSHEET

1. Project Title:

2. Funding Source Selected:

3. The Approach Most Likely to Meet with Success (based on research and contact with funding source):

4. Grant Request Size (range):

5. Evaluation Criteria or Points Assigned to Each of the Following Parts of the Proposal and Page Limitations for Each Component:

    a.   Need Statement —

    b.   Methods/Activities —

    c.   Evaluation —

    d.   Background of Principal Investigator/Project Director —

    e.   Attachments —

Document need by using statistics from articles and research, quotes from leaders or experts in the field, case statements, and statements from community people. It may also be effective to describe national need and reduce it to a local number that is more understandable and powerful.

The grants office's role in this process is to encourage the grant seeker to use all existing resources to search for relevant literature. Such resources include ERIC Searches, Dialog, and dissertation abstracts.

OBJECTIVES

Since on occasion the grants office will be asked to help a grant seeker to develop proposal objectives and methods, the office should have subject material on these areas.

Objectives are measurable steps taken to narrow or close the gap between what is and what ought to be. Objectives must follow the needs statement, since you cannot write an objective unless the need is documented.

To write an objective, you must first determine the results area, measurement indicators, performance standards, time frame, and cost frame, and then combine all of this information into a standard format. The standard format for a non-research objective is "To (action verb and statement reflecting your measurement indicator) by (performance standard) by (deadline) at a cost of no more than (cost frame)." For example, "To reduce hospital readmissions of people over sixty-five in Boise by 10 percent by the seventh month of the project at a cost of no more than $15,000."

A well-written objective reflects the amount of change wanted in a result area. If an objective does not reflect the amount of change desired, chances are that the measurement indicator is wrong or the performance standards are too low. Remember, objectives should emphasize the end results (the ultimate benefit of the program's work), not tasks or methods.

METHODS

The methods or activities section of a proposal is the detailed description of what will actually be done to meet the objectives. The methods section should:

- describe the program activities in detail

- describe the sequence, flow, and interrelationships of the activities

- describe the planned staffing of the program

- describe the client population and the method of determining client selection

- present a reasonable scope of activities that can be accomplished within the stated time frame and with the resources of the organization

It should also:

- make reference to the cost/benefit ratio of the project

- discuss why success is probable

- describe the uniqueness of the methods and overall project design

- assign responsibility to specific individuals for each part of the project

By encouraging grant seekers to use the project planner discussed in the following section, the grants office can be sure that the methods section will reflect a well-conceived plan for the accomplishment of the objectives.

Project Planner

You may decide to use a project planner to assist the proposal writer in developing the relationship between the objectives of his or her proposal and the methods/activities. The project planner was developed in my grants office at a university to assist me in understanding the grant writer's intentions and in developing a format that would lead to a realistic budget.

The project planner forces the grant writer to establish a relationship between the project personnel, space, equipment, consulting expense, and supplies and each method or activity proposed to meet each objective. Such task analysis allows the grants-office administrator to help the writer to negotiate the final award and administer the funded proposal.

The project planner allows you to develop quarterly cash forecasts, document in-kind or matching commitment, and monitor milestones or progress indicators. Whether these tasks fall under the purview of your grants office or not, the project planner outlines the key areas that will enhance your organization's credibility with the funder.

Review the following Project Planner Instructions on how to complete a project planner and develop an example that is tailored to your nonprofit organization and your fiscal system. Reproduce the instructions and your example, and distribute them to your prospective grant seekers to assist them in understanding their proposal, the budget, and the importance of demonstrating to the funding source that their project is organized and that the proposed results are attainable. The project planner also helps to make your organization appear capable of administering the funds after the award is made.

Pads of project planners are available from David G. Bauer Associates, Inc. Please use the order form at the end of the book.

Budget and Cash Forecasts

Grants offices usually assist grant seekers with budget preparation. Many potential problems can be avoided by establishing and implementing standardized budget procedures.

The grants office can help the grant seeker estimate costs accurately and save time by developing files on common grant-related costs, such as:

- phone installation

- office complement or setup

- indirect costs

- rental and lease agreements on common grant equipment

- square-footage costs

- security costs

Estimating salary and wages may be especially difficult because many nonprofits have relatively secret salary scales. Since staff members are often donated, the problem of secret salaries is compounded when the funding source requires the grantee to provide a matching or in-kind contribution. To combat this problem somewhat, list time requirements when developing your project planner, but avoid filling

PROJECT PLANNER INSTRUCTIONS

1. List your objectives or tasks in Column A. Not all funding sources are interested in particularly well-written objectives. Just give them what they want. Some contracts require tasks or enabling objectives.
2. In Column B, list the activities or methods necessary to meet the objective. These are the tasks that will meet the need.
3. In Column C/D, place the date you will begin the task and the date you will end it.
4. In Column E, designate the number of person weeks needed to accomplish the task. You may use person hours, person days, or person months instead.
5. Use Column F to designate the personnel that will spend measurable or significant amounts of time on the task. The determination of key personnel is critical for the development of job descriptions. By listing the activities or tasks that the key personnel are responsible for and the minimum qualifications or background required, you will have a job description. Call a placement agency to get an estimate of the salary needed to fill the position. The number of weeks or months of work will determine whether the position is part- or full-time.

   By completing this portion of the project planner, you will be able to quickly assess how many hours of work are assigned to a given time span. If you have your key personnel working more than 160 hours a month, you may need to change Column E—the number of person weeks necessary to accomplish the task.
6. Columns G, H, and I are for personnel costs. Special care should be taken to determine whose time on your staff (or in your organization) will be donated. This may be a requirement for the grant (refer back to the section on matching funds), or you may want to use this contribution to demonstrate your good faith to the funding source.

   Put an asterisk (*) by each person you donate to the project and be sure to include the donation of fringes for each person with donated wages.
7. Columns J, K, and L are for consultants and contract services. These three columns should be used for services that are most cost efficiently supplied by individuals who are not in your organization's normal employ. Note that there are no fringes paid to these individuals.
8. Columns M, N, O, and P are where you list the nonpersonnel resources needed to complete each activity and achieve your objective. Be careful not to underestimate the materials and supplies necessary for the successful completion of the project. Grant seekers sometimes lose out on potential donated or matching items simply because they do not ask themselves what they *really* need to complete each activity.

9. Column Q can be completed in one of two ways. Each activity can be subtotaled or several activities can be subtotaled together within each objective. In either case, lines should be drawn designating amounts requested, amounts donated, and total amounts so that the funding source can clearly see the in-kind contributions.

10. Under Column R, Milestones, record what the funding source will receive as progress indicators. Progress indicators should show the funding source that you are working toward your objectives.

11. Column S lists the date on which the funding source will receive the milestone or progress indicator.

12. INDIRECT COSTS—At the bottom of the project planner you will see a section on indirect costs. Indirect costs are usually a critical part of federal grants. Unfortunately, they are often poorly understood by *many* grant seekers. The concept involves repaying the recipient of a federal grant for costs that are indirectly attributable to the grant but are difficult to break down individually. Indirect costs are calculated by using a formula that is provided by the Federal Regional Controller's Office and include such things as:

    • heat and lights for an office
    • upkeep of the building
    • maintenance staff
    • the payroll department

    The formula is expressed as a percentage of the total amount requested from the funding source (represented as _____ % T.D.C. $\times$ Box T on the project planner) or as a percentage of the people on the grant (represented as _____ % Salaries and Wages $\times$ Box U on the project planner).

PROJECT PLANNER

PROJECT TITLE: _____

A. List Project objectives or outcomes A. B. B. List Methods to accomplish each objective as A-1, A-2, A-3 . . . B-1, B-2 . . .	MONTH		TIME	PROJECT PERSONNEL	PERSONNEL COSTS		
	BEGIN	END			SALARIES & WAGES	FRINGE BENEFITS	TOTAL
	C / D		E	F	G	H	I

TOTAL DIRECT COSTS OR COSTS REQUESTED FROM FUNDER ▶

MATCHING FUNDS, IN-KIND CONTRIBUTIONS, OR DONATED COSTS ▶

TOTAL COSTS ▶

Proposal Developed for _____

PROJECT DIRECTOR: _____ Proposed starting date _____ Proposal Year _____

CONSULTANTS • CONTRACT SERVICES			NON-PERSONNEL RESOURCES NEEDED SUPPLIES • EQUIPMENT • MATERIALS				SUB-TOTAL COST FOR ACTIVITY	MILESTONES PROGRESS INDICATORS	
TIME	COST/WEEK	TOTAL	ITEM	COST/ITEM	QUANTITY	TOT. COST	TOTAL I. L. P	ITEM	DATE
J	K	L	M	N	O	P	Q	R	S

						T		◄ % OF TOTAL
								◄
								◄ **107**
							100%	◄

GRANTS OFFICE TIME LINE

ACTIV- ITY NO.	1	2	3	4	5	6	7	8	9	10	11	12	TOTAL COST FOR ACTIVITY

1st QUARTER		2nd QUARTER		3rd QUARTER		4th QUARTER		TOTAL

QUARTERLY FORECAST OF EXPENDITURES ▲

in the salary and wages column until the proposal is ready to be submitted to the funding source.

Although budget requirements and forms vary, the basic information required is generally the same. Careful construction of your project planner will help you prepare your budget with a cost estimate for each activity. However, remember that your project planner is not the budget—it is an analysis of what has to be done and the costs involved in each step of the process.

The Grants Time Line

The Grants Office Time Line is an invaluable tool. It will help to maintain the organization's image and credibility with the grantor by providing an understanding of the relationship between activities and their timing. It will also assist the grants administrator in meeting the milestones (progress indicators) listed on columns R and S of the project planner.

The grants administrator should have a copy of the time line of each grant in progress. In addition, the project director or principal investigator should have a copy of the time line on his or her wall. This will help to avoid problems such as late reporting and overlooked reports, which can severely damage the grantee's credibility with the prospective funder.

The Budget For Public Funding Sources

Public funding sources typically require that several detailed budget sheets be submitted in the source's own specific format. Generally, the budget section is located several sections away from the objectives and methodology sections. To assist you in budget negotiation and for other reasons already discussed, complete a project planner and use it to develop the budget. Place the figures developed into whatever format is requested by the funder.

The following budget forms, Part III—Budget Information and Section C–Non-Federal Resources, are used for several federal programs. However, when completing a budget for a specific program you must use the forms provided in the particular agency's proposal-guideline package.

You may retrieve the information requested on the budget summary and budget categories from your project planner.

Use your Grants Office Time Line to develop the required information on cash forecast. Each activity or method has a project

OMB No.: 1121-0012

PART III — BUDGET INFORMATION

SECTION A — BUDGET SUMMARY

Grant Program, Function or Activity (a)	Federal Catalog No. (b)	Estimated Unobligated Funds		New or Revised Budget		
		Federal (c)	Non-Federal (d)	Federal (e)	Non-Federal (f)	Total (g)
1.		$	$	$	$	$
2.						
3.						
4.						
5. TOTALS		$	$	$	$	$

SECTION B — BUDGET CATEGORIES

6. Object Class Categories	Grant Program, Function or Activity				Total (5)
	(1)	(2)	(3)	(4)	
a. Personnel	$	$	$	$	$
b. Fringe Benefits					
c. Travel					
d. Equipment					
e. Supplies					
f. Contractual					
g. Construction					
h. Other					
i. Total Direct Charges					
j. Indirect Charges					
k. TOTALS	$	$	$	$	$
7. Program Income	$	$	$	$	$

OJARS Form 4000/3 (Rev. 6-81)
Attachment to SF-424

110

OMB No.: 1121-0012

SECTION C — NON-FEDERAL RESOURCES

(a) Grant Program	(b) APPLICANT	(c) STATE	(d) OTHER SOURCES	(e) TOTALS
8.	$	$	$	$
9.				
10.				
11.				
12. TOTALS	$	$	$	$

SECTION D — FORECASTED CASH NEEDS

	Total for 1st Year	1st Quarter	2nd Quarter	3rd Quarter	4th Quarter
13. Federal	$	$	$	$	$
14. Non-Federal					
15. TOTAL	$	$	$	$	$

SECTION E — BUDGET ESTIMATES OF FEDERAL FUNDS NEEDED FOR BALANCE OF THE PROJECT

(a) Grant Program	FUTURE FUNDING PERIODS (YEARS)			
	(b) FIRST	(c) SECOND	(d) THIRD	(e) FOURTH
16.	$	$	$	$
17.				
18.				
19.				
20. TOTALS	$	$	$	$

SECTION F — OTHER BUDGET INFORMATION

(Attach Additional Sheets If Necessary)

21. Direct Charges:

22. Indirect Charges:

23. Remarks:

OJARS Form 4000/3 (Rev. 6-81)
Attachment to SF-424

111

begin and end date. You can also determine the cost of each activity or method by adding together the cost of all the elements needed to complete the activity. With a little extrapolation on the cost of each activity and when it will begin and end, you can get a rough idea of the quarterly cash flow.

The Budget for Private Funding Sources

Budget formats for private funding sources will vary widely. Most foundations and corporations do not provide a suggested format. Some leave this item up to the discretion of the applicant; others do not require a budget at all—just the total amount requested.

You may use the format of the following Sample Project Budget in those instances when the funding source does not provide or suggest a format. If attachments are allowed, include a project planner in your proposal. This can be very beneficial, since space is often limited to two to five pages in the private proposal system and the project planner succinctly tells the whole story. The project planner explains the budget request (sometimes referred to as the budget narrative), and in some cases the planner may be viewed by private funding sources *as* the budget and budget narrative. It also appeals to those readers/reviewers who are visually oriented. A private funding source project planner with a section summarizing budget categories is available from David G. Bauer Associates, Inc.

An estimate of the cash forecast can be made from the Grants Office Time Line. Follow the same procedure as for federal funds.

Proposal-Improvement Committee

One of the most effective techniques for encouraging staff to produce proposals is to organize a proposal-improvement committee. The purpose of this committee is to increase the fundability of proposals by reviewing them in the same way that actual reviewers and board members will review them.

Research and preproposal contact should provide the information necessary to duplicate the real reviewing process. For example, if your research indicates an in-depth review process, you may want to send the committee members a draft of the proposal prior to the committee meeting with a note outlining the amount of time the

SAMPLE PROJECT BUDGET

Project Name:	Expen-diture Total	Donated/In-Kind	Requested From This Source
I. PERSONNEL			
A. Salaries, Wages			
B. Fringe Benefits			
C. Consultants/Contracted Service			
PERSONNEL SUBTOTAL			

SAMPLE PROJECT BUDGET (cont'd.)

Project Name:	Expen-diture Total	Donated/ In-Kind	Requested From This Source
II. NONPERSONNEL			
A. Space Costs			
B. Equipment			
C. Supplies (Consumables)			
D. Travel Local Out of Town			
E. Telephone			

SAMPLE PROJECT BUDGET (cont'd.)

Project Name:	Expen- diture Total	Donated/ In-Kind	Requested From This Source
F. Other Nonpersonnel Costs			
NONPERSONNEL SUBTOTAL:			
PERSONNEL SUBTOTAL:			
PROJECT TOTAL:			
PERCENTAGE:			

NOTES:

reviewers actually spend on each proposal and a sketch of their backgrounds. (However, please note that you will most often review the research on the funding source and the time limitations for the review at committee meetings since many proposals are reviewed in less than one hour.)

The proposal-improvement committee should comprise your most promising grant writers. I initiated the idea of an improvement committee by inviting potential members to my grants office for lunch. I explained the activities of the committee to them and assured everyone present that the meetings would not last longer than one hour and would include a free lunch. After several months of meetings and a rotation of committee members, former committee members were actually organizing their own committees.

The greatest impetus for the use and acceptance of my idea came when several letter proposals to private funders, each less than five pages long, received funding. Committee members and staff began to feel that if these proposals could bring in money, so could theirs. They also learned that the background of reviewers, as well as writing style and proposal organization, were important factors in the process that could not be forgotten in the zeal to tell the funding source what he or she *wanted*.

In summary, the implementation of a proposal-improvement committee can:

- result in a greater sensitivity and understanding of the funding source's values

- increase the number and quality of the proposals that come from the members of the committee

- foster a positive atmosphere for suggesting proposal improvements and reduce the negative, fault-finding atmosphere that a proposal-critiquing exercise can often produce

The following three worksheets should be used by the proposal-improvement committee. They are:

- the Proposal-Improvement Committee Worksheet, which explains the task of the committee and the proposal-review procedure

- the Proposal-Improvement Committee—Funder Profile

- the Proposal-Improvement Committee Scoring Worksheet

PROPOSAL-IMPROVEMENT COMMITTEE WORKSHEET

Thank you for assisting us in our efforts to produce quality proposals that enhance our organization's image. Your task is to review each proposal and identify those elements that are positive, and should be retained in the final version of the proposal, and those elements that need to be improved. Your suggestions for improving the weak areas would be appreciated.

It is critical to the success of this exercise and ultimately to the acceptance of this proposal that you review it from a viewpoint that closely matches that of the real reviewer's. To assist you in this task, we have included a summary of our research on the prospective funders. Remember, please make your suggestions from the funder's point of view!

Instructions

- Review the funding-source description and role-play how you would see our proposal from their eyes.

- Read the proposal and indicate with a plus (+) those elements you feel may be appealing to the funding source.

- Indicate with a minus (−) those elements that might be viewed negatively by the funding source.

Since we are simulating the way in which this proposal will be read by this funding source, please follow the time constraints that our research has uncovered. Remember, the funders do not always pore over every word. Although some spend several hours, most skim the proposal in ten minutes.

PROPOSAL-IMPROVEMENT COMMITTEE— FUNDER PROFILE

PROPOSAL TITLE: _____

PROSPECTIVE FUNDING SOURCE: _____

AREAS OF INTEREST TO FUNDING SOURCE:

SAMPLES OF GRANTS IN INTEREST AREAS:

PROPOSAL REVIEW PROCEDURE

PROPOSALS ARE
READ BY:

	X	TIME	EDUCATIONAL BACKGROUND	SOCIO/ECON. BACKGROUND	KNOWN BIASES OR VIEWPOINTS	OTHER
FUNDING OFFICIAL						
FUNDING STAFF						
REVIEW COMMITTEES						
BOARD MEMBERS						
OTHER						

GENERAL FUNDING SOURCE INFORMATION

NUMBER OF PROPOSALS RECEIVED IN 19 __ : _____

NUMBER FUNDED IN 19 __ : _____

AMOUNT OF $ DISTRIBUTED IN 19 __ : _____

ANTICIPATED DISTRIBUTION OF $ IN 19 __ : _____

APPLICATION PROCESS & GUIDELINES

PROPOSAL REVIEWED
        (MONTHLY, QUARTERLY, ANNUALLY, AS NEEDED): _____

PROPOSAL FORMAT AND LENGTH:

ATTACHMENTS ALLOWED:

OTHER:

PROPOSAL-IMPROVEMENT COMMITTEE— FUNDER PROFILE

PROPOSAL TITLE: __**METROPOLITAN HOSPICE**__

PROSPECTIVE FUNDING SOURCE: __**CALDWELL FOUNDATION**__

AREAS OF INTEREST TO FUNDING SOURCE:
HOSPTIALS/HEALTH CARE
COLLEGES/UNIVERSITIES (EDUCATION)

SAMPLES OF GRANTS IN INTEREST AREAS:
$15,000 to METRO HOSPITAL FOR NEW EMERGENCY ROOM ADDITION
$10,000 to JONES COLLEGE FOR BUSINESS SCHOOL

PROPOSAL REVIEW PROCEDURE

PROPOSALS ARE READ BY:

	X	TIME	EDUCATIONAL BACKGROUND	SOCIO/ECON. BACKGROUND	KNOWN BIASES OR VIEWPOINTS	OTHER
FUNDING OFFICIAL						
FUNDING STAFF						
REVIEW COMMITTEES						
BOARD MEMBERS	X	5–10 mins.	B.S Degrees M.B.A	Upper Class	Like to help people and themselves	
OTHER						

GENERAL FUNDING SOURCE INFORMATION

NUMBER OF PROPOSALS RECEIVED IN 19 **86** : __150__

NUMBER FUNDED IN 19 **86** : __12__

AMOUNT OF $ DISTRIBUTED IN 19 **86** : __$250,000__

ANTICIPATED DISTRIBUTION OF $ IN 19 **87** : __$260,000__

APPLICATION PROCESS & GUIDELINES

PROPOSAL REVIEWED
(MONTHLY, QUARTERLY, ANNUALLY, AS NEEDED): __**AS NEEDED**__

PROPOSAL FORMAT AND LENGTH:
1 PAGE LETTER PROPOSAL

ATTACHMENTS ALLOWED: **NONE**

OTHER:

PROPOSAL-IMPROVEMENT COMMITTEE SCORING WORKSHEET

Instructions: Complete a scoring worksheet for the positive areas identified and another for the areas needing improvement. Select a committee secretary to do the recording. Put the committee members' initials on both sheets in the boxes provided. On the first sheet, list all of the positive areas. After all of the positive areas are listed, have each committee member assign points to each one. Each committee member has a total of ten points to use. The more points awarded to a particular area, the more strongly it is liked. After each committee member is done scoring the areas, the secretary should total the points for each area. The greater the points, the higher the rank, the more positive the area. Do the same on a worksheet for the areas needing improvement. The more points awarded to an area, the more needy it is.

Circle One: Positive Areas/Areas to Improve

LIST AREAS IDENTIFIED	INITIALS								TOTAL POINTS PER AREA	RANK
INDIVIDUAL TOTAL									GROUP TOTAL	

GRANTS OFFICE INVENTORY
Chapter 7
The Role of the Grants Office in Promoting an Organized Proposal

For Each Activity/Item Listed, Check Status:

Activity/Item	Reviewed, Appropriate Part of Grants Office	Reviewed, Appropriate Part of Other Office (List)	Reviewed, Not Applicable	Reviewed, Inappropriate Needs Action	Non-existent, Needs Action
1. Grants office procedure manual—suggestions, forms and worksheets for: • organizing proposal ideas (swiss cheese concept, workbook, etc.) • writing needs statements, objectives and methods					

Complete this Section for Each Activity/Item Needing Action:

What Needs to Be Accomplished? (Activity/Item)	By Whom? (Office/Person)	By When? (Time Frame)	Resources, Required—Personnel, Supplies, Equipment, Programming, etc.	Estimated Costs

GRANTS OFFICE INVENTORY

Chapter 7 (continued)

The Role of the Grants Office in Promoting an Organized Proposal

For Each Activity/Item Listed, Check Status:

Activity/Item	Reviewed, Appropriate Part of Grants Office	Reviewed, Appropriate Part of Other Office (List)	Reviewed, Not Applicable	Reviewed, Inappropriate Needs Action	Non-existent, Needs Action
• tailoring proposals to funding sources (tailoring worksheet) • developing budgets and budget formats (project planner) • estimating cash forecasts (time line) 2. Proposal improvement committee (or other system for re-					

Complete this Section for Each Activity/Item Needing Action:

What Needs to Be Accomplished? (Activity/Item)	By Whom? (Office/Person)	By When? (Time Frame)	Resources, Required— Personnel, Supplies, Equipment, Programming, etc.	Estimated Costs

GRANTS OFFICE INVENTORY
Chapter 7 (continued)
The Role of the Grants Office in Promoting an Organized Proposal

For Each Activity/Item Listed, Check Status:

Activity/Item	Reviewed, Appropriate Part of Grants Office	Reviewed, Appropriate Part of Other Office (List)	Reviewed, Not Applicable	Reviewed, Inappropriate Needs Action	Non-existent, Needs Action
viewing proposals in the same manner the actual reviewers will review them prior to submittal)					

Complete this Section for Each Activity/Item Needing Action:

What Needs to Be Accomplished? (Activity/Item)	By Whom? (Office/ Person)	By When? (Time Frame)	Resources, Required— Personnel, Supplies, Equipment, Programming, etc.	Estimated Costs

CHAPTER 8

The Role of the Grants Office in Assurances, Submission, and Follow-Up

Grants offices usually assist in proposal preparation by providing support services such as editing, typing, budget assistance, and so on. Most, however, do not actually write the proposals for the staff. Professionals in the grants field agree that the best approach to grant writing is to have the expert in the subject area write the proposal.

In the smaller grants office, or in the decentralized system, actual grant writing may be performed in the grants office. While writing the proposal for the grant seeker is not advised, it may be a necessary step in the development of the skills and confidence of the staff. In this case, the grants office's assistance should be viewed as educational, and it must be understood that the assistance is only a transitory step meant to teach the staff about grant writing. This way, the grants office will eventually be free to allocate time to other important aspects of grant seeking, such as assurances, protection of human subjects, sign-off procedures, recording and monitoring of matching funds, proposal submission, and follow-up with public and private funding sources.

Assurances

The grants office assures government funding sources that all rules, guidelines, and stipulations have been followed. Every grants office should have a checklist of assurances for each type of funding source. The appropriate individuals and offices should review the checklist and sign off on the assurances as they are met. The responsible individuals should receive special instructions to make sure that the office has complied with certain rules. For example, it should be noted if the personnel office must comply with assurances regarding the manner in which job openings are advertised, fair employment procedures followed, and positions filled. The grants office is the logical choice for informing individuals and offices within the organization of their particular responsibilities in dealing with the funders' restrictions.

In some nonprofit organizations the business office or accounting department may control purchasing of supplies, materials, or equipment. Federal and state grants and contracts are known for their rules and regulations in this area. In addition to rules on requiring bids on purchases, there are assurances that the grantee allow minority businesses to compete. If the business office does not sign off on the proposal, or see the checklist of assurances, the nonprofit may inadvertently be in violation of these rules.

Block-grant recipients, who accept federal pass-through dollars, sign assurances that they will treat the administration of the funds as if the ultimate grantee received the funds directly from the federal government. (In the early 1980s, many categorical federal programs were condensed into block grants, or pass-through monies, and given to states for distribution.) This means that the recipients must abide by the federal rules that govern the purchase, rental, and lease of equipment; personnel practices; record keeping, and so on.

Unfortunately, many nonprofit organizations deal with the area of assurances only after there is a problem, for example, when a federal audit reveals a large error in the administration of funds. *Remember,* pleading ignorance is no excuse. Proper education by the grants office will result in a planned, preventive system that will maintain the organization's present and future credibility.

A partial Checklist of Assurances and Approvals is provided at the end of this section so you can review assurances that apply to grants. Send for information from the Office of Management and Budget Circulars to add other appropriate assurances to your list. Reproduce the list for your grants office's use.

CHECKLIST OF ASSURANCES
AND APPROVALS*

Regulations/Assurance/Approval	In Files
Employment/Labor	
Accessibility for Handicapped	_____
Civil Rights Act 1964	_____
Davis Bacon Prevailing Wage Act	_____
Equal Opportunity Act Affirmative Action	_____
Fair Labor Standards Act	_____
Hatch Act (Political Activity of Employees)	_____
Historical	
Historic Preservation Act	_____
Historical and Archeological Data Preservation Act	_____
Contract/Grant Administration	
Copeland Anti-Kickback	_____
Minority Contractors Act	_____
Patents & Copyrights	_____
Environmental Protection	
Federal Water Pollution Control Act	_____
Safe Drinking Water Act	_____
Wild and Scenic Rivers Act	_____
Endangered Species Act	_____
Freedom of Information 5 U.S. Code 552	_____
Privacy Act 5 U.S. Code 552A	_____

* See Chapter 11 for other assurances.

OFFICE OF MANAGEMENT AND BUDGET (OMB) CIRCULARS

A–21   Principles for Determining Costs Applicable to Grants, Contracts, and Other Agreements with Educational Institutions.
2/26/79 and revision 12/2/86 (50 Pages)

A–87   Cost Principles for State and Local Governments.
1/28/81 (8 Pages)

A–88   Indirect Cost Rates, Audit and Audit Follow-Up at Educational Institutions.
12/5/79 (10 Pages)

A–102   Grants and Cooperative Agreements with State and Local Governments.
3/3/88 (8 Pages)

A–110   Grants and Agreements with Institutions of Higher Education, Hospitals, and other Non-Profit Organizations.
7/30/76 revision 2/10/87 (27 Pages)

A–122   Cost Principles for Non-Profit Organizations.
4/8/80 (11 Pages), Notice 4/27/84 (20 Pages)

A–128   Audits of State and Local Governments.
4/12/85 (13 Pages), Notice 11/13/87 (8 Pages)

Ethics in Research
by Mary L. Otto

After World War II the federal government became the major funding source for research in the United States. Federal agencies were created and authorized by Congress to award research funds to nonprofit organizations. Over the years these agencies have broadened their scope to include monitoring of ethical standards for research. Institutions that receive funds from federal agencies are required to adhere to all federal, state, and local statutes, as well as agency policies governing research projects.

Specific guidelines regulating the conditions of research at institutions of higher education have been issued by the Public Health Service (PHS), the Food and Drug Administration (FDA), and the National Institutes of Health (NIH). All of these agencies work under the auspices of the U.S. Department of Health and Human Services (DHHS). Other federal and state funding agencies accept the DHHS, PHS, and NIH guidelines as the standard requirements for research. These guidelines stipulate minimal criteria and are not intended to deter a college or university from establishing more stringent regulations or from adhering to additional professional or legal guidelines.

The university's research office is responsible for ensuring that research proposals submitted to external agencies comply with all federal, state, and local statutes governing the research. Regulations and laws generally apply to the use of human subjects, laboratory research animals, recombinant DNA molecules, and hazardous substances.

The research administrative unit at colleges and universities is required to establish procedures to ensure that all of the applicable federal, state, and local regulations are met during the research process. Those institutions seeking external funding to support research must also meet the requirements of the funding agency.

Most colleges and universities have a single set of review criteria with a separate review committee for each regulated area to promote the same ethical standards for all research, whether externally or internally funded. The same review process provides consistent procedures for all research and eases record keeping for the research administration office.

Although the multiple review of proposed research projects by a variety of committees may seem to create an unnecessary layer of bureaucratic paperwork, the reviews are vehicles for ensuring that ethical consideration is given to each aspect of the research, thus improving the overall quality. Numerous incidents have been cited that demonstrate past disregard for the ethical issues in research. To ensure that research questions do not take precedence over safety and ethical issues, projects must be designed to provide protection from risks.

INTERNAL REVIEW

The proposal review process begins with the institution's internal review of the proposal. The internal review form should be designed by the research office for each college or university to meet the institution's needs. The form typically specifies the institution's willingness to participate in the research project. Oakland University's (Rochester, Michigan) Approval of Application for External Grant or Contract form provides an example of the type of information that can be required for an internal review.

When authorizing applications for external funds, universities must be prepared to make commitments for matching funds, tuition remission, and space for the project. To reduce confusion over what commitments have been made and who is to provide resources once a project is funded, the internal review requires the approval of the person in charge of resources. The review also provides a permanent record so the research office can keep track of commitments. This form is not sent to the funding agency.

In addition to spelling out university commitments, the internal review requires department chairs and deans to approve the project, thus ensuring that the principal investigator or program director will be available to work on the project. Since awards are made to colleges or universities, not to individuals, the institution is responsible to the funding agency and must be prepared to honor its personnel, financial, and space commitments for funded projects.

INSTITUTIONAL ANIMAL CARE AND USE REVIEW

The Office for Protection from Research Risks of the National Institutes of Health has issued the *Public Health Service Policy on Humane Care and Use of Laboratory Animals*. This document requires that institutions establish protocol to ensure appropriate care and use of all animals involved in research, research training, and biological testing activities conducted or supported by the PHS. It also requires that institutions submit an assurance of compliance statement to PHS.

OAKLAND UNIVERSITY

APPROVAL OF APPLICATION FOR EXTERNAL GRANT OR CONTRACT

Type of Proposal
(check one)

_____ community service
_____ faculty fellowship
_____ graduate assistantship
_____ instructional
_____ research
_____ student service/support

Status of Application
(check one)

_____ new application
_____ non-competing renewal
_____ (continuation)
_____ competing renewal

1. Project Personnel:
   a. Project Director _____
      (name) _____ Department
   b. Co-Director _____
      (name) _____ Department
   c. Other participating
      faculty and staff _____
      (name) _____ Department
      _____
      (name) _____ Department
      _____
      (name) _____ Department
   d. Student Participants _____
      (number of students) _____ Undergraduate
      _____
      (number of students) _____ Graduate

2. Project Title: _____

3. Funding Source/Submission Date: _____

4. Project budget: (University support requires signature of person responsible for accounts.)
   a. Amount requested from sponsor $ _____
   b. University support
      Salary (acct. no. _____) $ _____ Approval
      Equipment (acct. no. _____) $ _____ Approval
      Tuition Waiver (acct. no. _____) $ _____ Approval
      Other _____
            (acct. no. _____) $ _____ Approval
   c. Graduate Assistants: (check appropriate source)
      _____ existing departmental allocation $ _____ Approval
      _____ new department allocation $ _____ Approval
      _____ new allocation/Graduate Dean $ _____ Approval
   d. TOTAL PROJECT COST $ _____

— continued on back —

5. Does this project involve:

	Yes	No	Date of Approval
a. Use of radioactive materials	_____	_____	_____
b. Research on human subjects	_____	_____	_____
c. Animal experimentation	_____	_____	_____
d. Recombinant DNA	_____	_____	_____

6. University facilities required:
   a. Will adequate space be available for the project? _____ yes _____ no
      If yes, building _____ room #(s) _____
      If no, space required _____ sq. ft.
      Source _____ Approval _____
   b. Space renovation $ _____
      O.U. account no. _____ Approval _____
   c. Will acquisition of equipment require installation and/or building modification at cost to the University?
      _____ yes _____ no
      If yes, approval _____

7. Additional information: _____

8. Signatures: (Required prior to proposal approval by the Director of Research & Academic Development)

   (1) _____   (Project Director)   Date _____
   (2) _____   (Department Chairperson)   Date _____
   (3) _____   (Dean/Director)   Date _____
   (4) _____   (Grants Administrator)   Date _____

The statement must be approved and the institution issued an assurance number, which is required on proposals to all PHS agencies.

The policy requires that any institution conducting research funded by PHS must have an institutional animal care and use committee (IACUC), appointed by the president or chief executive officer of the institution. This committee must consist of a veterinarian, one active scientist, one community member with no affiliation to the institution, and one nonscientist. More than one role can be filled by any individual committee member, but the committee is not to be made up of fewer than five individuals. The IACUC is charged with reviewing all protocols for using animals in research. Each investigator is required to submit information on animal use to the IACUC and receive approval prior to beginning any research involving animals or submitting a proposal requesting external funds.

The IACUC reviews only the protocol involving the use of animals. It may approve the project as submitted or request that the investigator make changes in the protocol. The IACUC is primarily concerned that the research avoid unnecessary discomfort, pain, or anxiety to the animal. The committee also must consider whether the anticipated results will be for the good of society, whether the work will be performed by a qualified scientist, and whether the appropriate species has been chosen for this particular research project.

In general, the IACUC is a collegial group working with the scientist to ensure the best possible protocol for the research project, thus protecting the animal's welfare without interfering with the design of the research. The IACUC works with the investigator to make appropriate changes when desired rather than inhibiting or stopping a research project. However, if it is not possible to reach an agreeable solution, the IACUC is authorized to prohibit the research.

Once a project has been approved, the IACUC monitors the research through visits to the laboratories. Investigators may not make any changes in protocol without first receiving the permission of the IACUC.

Any college or university seeking external funds for research involving animals will probably establish its own IACUC. However, if only a few projects are being conducted on the campus, it is permissible to have research projects reviewed by a PHS approved IACUC at another university, research institution, or hospital. All proposals requesting external funds must have a letter signed by the chair of an approved IACUC indicating approval of the project before funds will be awarded for the research.

In addition to requiring IACUC approval of research, the PHS policy also requires that institutions appoint an animal assurance officer, who is ultimately responsible for maintaining compliance. In medium-size institutions, the assurance officer is likely to be a qualified faculty administrator who works in the research administration office. A full-time veterinarian, if available, is desirable for the position.

The Oakland University Notice of Intent to Use Vertebrate Animals in Research or Instruction is an example of the kind of information needed for an IACUC review. It was designed for a medium-size university that uses animals in several research projects but does not use either large animals or primates.

INSTITUTIONAL REVIEW/HUMAN SUBJECTS IN RESEARCH

The review of the use of human subjects in research is designed to protect these subjects while promoting science and social welfare. Disregard for human subjects generally occurs because the researcher believes the potential outcome of the research is worth taking the risk. However, in spite of the possible gain, participants must be fully informed about the research and freely consent to be involved before they can be used as subjects.

The Office for Protection from Research Risks, NIH, and the associate commissioner for health affairs, FDA, have issued the *Official IRB Guidebook,* which outlines the specific requirements of institutions engaging in research using human subjects.* This guidebook includes special guidelines protecting children and other vulnerable populations from involuntary or inappropriate use as research subjects.

The office of research is required to submit an assurance of compliance with the approved guidelines for the use of human subjects in research to DHHS. The institution receives a multiple-project assurance code, which is required on all proposals involving human subjects. Colleges and universities are also required to establish an institutional review board (IRB) for the use of human subjects in research to review research protocols of all projects that use human subjects. The IRB must include two physicians, at least one psychologist, and one person with no affiliation to the institution, and it must include individuals of both gender. An IRB with this makeup may approve medical or psychological research protocols. The review of research protocols by the IRB focuses on possible risk of physical, psychological, or social injury to participants resulting from the research. If there are any apparent risks, the participants must receive adequate protection and the potential benefits to them and to hu-

* Other reference documents include OPRR Reports—Protection of Human Subjects (45CFR46) and the Belmont Report.

OAKLAND UNIVERSITY
NOTICE OF INTENT TO USE VERTEBRATE ANIMALS IN
RESEARCH OR INSTRUCTION

Date _____

Principal Investigator/Course Director _____

Highest Degree Held _____

Department _____

Number of Project, Grant or Course (if applicable) _____

Project/Course Title _____

Project/Course Period _____ to _____

1. Please estimate the starting and ending dates of the project/course

Species to be used	Total number of animals to be used	Number of animals to be housed/day	Number of days animals will be housed

2. Where will the animals be housed:

Building(s) _____

Room Number(s) _____

Off campus site(s) _____

3. Duration of housing requirement(s) for animals (please check)

Short term (5 days or less) _____

Long term (more than 5 days) _____

Both short and long term _____

4. Source(s) of animals; identify vendor(s) or breeder(s) _____

5. (a) Identify the faculty member(s) responsible for the standards of animal husbandry and housing (if other than the principal investigator). _____

(b) Identify the technical staff member(s) responsible for observing animals daily and reporting ill or injured animals. _____

6. Identify or describe the restraint system(s) for animals that may be required for this research or instruction (e.g., restraint chairs, collars, vests, harnesses, slings). _____

7. (a) Identify or describe all nonsurgical manipulations or procedures involving the animals in the order in which they will be performed. _____

(b) Where will these procedures be performed?

Building(s) _____

Room Number(s) _____

Off campus site(s) _____

(c) Specify the drug(s), dose(s), route(s) of administration or other methods to be used in alleviating significant pain or discomfort. If pain relieving drugs will not be used, please explain why. _____

(continued)

8. (a) If surgery is involved in this research or instruction, identify or describe the surgical procedure(s) _____

_____

(b) Identify the faculty or staff member(s) who will perform the surgery (if other than the principal investigator) _____

(c) Where will the surgery be performed?

Building(s) _____

Room Number(s) _____

Off campus site(s) _____

(d) Identify or describe the pre-operative preparation procedure(s) and anesthetic method(s) including drug(s), dose(s) route(s) and supplementation schedules.

_____

_____

(e) Identify or describe the postsurgical monitoring and care procedure(s) to be used.

_____

_____

(f) Identify the individual(s) responsible for postsurgical monitoring and care of the animals (if other than the principal investigator).

_____

(g) Is normal eating, drinking, or physical movement likely to be impaired beyond the immediate postsurgical period? _____

If yes, 1) identify the expected abnormality and its duration, and 2) specify measures planned to assist the animals.

_____

_____

9. (a) Specify the method(s) of euthanasia. _____

(b) Identify the individual(s) who will perform euthanasia (if other than the principal investigator).

_____

10. (a) If the reason or instruction requires the use of hazardous agents (i.e., infectious agents, carcinogens, toxic chemicals, radioisotopes), specify the agent(s) to be used.

_____

(b) Specify the containment method(s) to followed in protecting other research animals and personnel from the hazardous agent(s)

_____

_____

_____

Principal Investigator/Course Director

Please return the completed form to:

134

mankind in general must be great enough to justify their participation in the project.

Some research projects involving human subjects are exempt from review. These include normal educational practices; educational tests when subjects are not identified; survey or interview procedures when the subjects are not identified and their privacy rites are protected; observations of public behavior when subject privacy rites are protected; collection or study of existing data, documents, records, or specimens when subjects are not identified and the information is publicly available; and public benefit or service programs, such as those under the Social Security Act.

Human subjects must sign a written, informed consent form approved by the IRB. The IRB may waive the requirement for a signed consent form if the form is the only record linking the subject to the research or if the research presents no more than minimal risk of harm to subjects and involves no procedures for which written consent is normally required outside of the research context. In all other cases, subjects must sign a consent form before participating in the research. To ensure that all subjects understand the nature of the research, the informed consent form must include a reasonable description of it. The form must state that participation is voluntary and that refusal to participate will not result in a penalty or loss of benefits to the subject. The detailed requirements for a consent form are described in the OPRR Reports and the *Official IRB Guidebook.*

The Consent Form Checklist used by investigators at Oakland University, adopted from one used at Northwestern University, is used to check consent forms before sending them to the IRB for approval. The checklist highlights the primary requirements for consent forms.

Before applying for external funds for a research project involving human subjects, the researcher must apply to the IRB and receive approval. The Oakland University Human Subjects Review Form for New or Periodic Review is an example of a form that provides to the IRB information on research projects at a university without a medical school.

The chair of the IRB works very closely with the research administration office. Often the chair is a staff member from the office. All proposals involving human subjects must include a letter approving the project signed by the IRB chair. Since projects can be approved for only one year, investigators must resubmit yearly for a new approval. The IRB's record keeping and correspondence system is quite extensive, so secretarial assistance must be provided for this committee.

OAKLAND UNIVERSITY
HUMAN SUBJECTS REVIEW FORM
FOR NEW OR PERIODIC REVIEW

PROJECT DIRECTOR(S): _____

FACULTY SPONSOR (if applicable): _____

SCHOOL: _____ DEPARTMENT: _____

PROJECT TITLE: _____

PROPOSED PROJECT DATES: _____

FUNDING AGENCY OR RESEARCH SPONSOR: _____

PROJECT DIRECTOR'S TELEPHONE NUMBER: _____

Please answer the questions below and return this form with a copy of the CURRENT CONSENT FORM to the Office of Research and Academic Development, 370 South Foundation Hall.

I. Project Information:
   A. Project activity STATUS is: (Check one of the four boxes, as appropriate.)
      ☐ NEW PROJECT
      ☐ NEW PROJECT qualifying for EXPEDITED REVIEW (eligibility requirements are specified on the back page.)
      ☐ PERIODIC REVIEW ON CONTINUING PROJECT
      ☐ PROCEDURAL REVISION TO PREVIOUSLY APPROVED PROJECT (Please indicate in the PROTOCOL section the way in which the project has been revised.)

   B. This project involves the use of an INVESTIGATIONAL NEW DRUG (IND) OR AN APPROVED DRUG FOR AN UNAPPROVED USE in or on human subjects.
      ☐ YES   ☐ NO
      Drug name, IND number and company: _____

   C. This project involves the use of an INVESTIGATIONAL MEDICAL DEVICE (IMD) or an APPROVED MEDICAL DEVICE FOR AN UNAPPROVED USE.
      ☐ YES   ☐ NO
      Device name, IMD number and company: _____

   D. This project involves the use of RADIATION or RADIOISOTOPES in or on human subjects.
      ☐ YES   ☐ NO

   E. This project involves the use of Oakland University students.
      ☐ YES   ☐ NO

   F. HUMAN SUBJECTS from the following population(s) would be involved in this study:
      ☐ Minors   ☐ Fetuses
      ☐ Abortuses   ☐ Pregnant Women
      ☐ Prisoners   ☐ Mentally Retarded
      ☐ Mentally Disabled ☐ None of the Above

   G. Total Number of Subjects to be Studied: _____

INSTITUTIONAL REVIEW BOARD
OFFICE OF RESEARCH & ACADEMIC DEVELOPMENT

EXPEDITED REVIEW APPLICATION

Research activities in which the only involvement of human subjects will be in one or more of the following categories may be reviewed by the Institutional Review Board through the expedited review procedure. Please indicate into which of the categories your research falls:

☐ 1) Collection of hair and nail clippings, in a nondisfiguring manner, deciduous teeth, and permanent teeth if care indicates a need for extraction.

☐ 2) Collection of excreta and external secretions including sweat, uncannulated saliva, placenta removed at delivery, and amniotic fluid at the time of rupture of the membrane prior to or during labor.

☐ 3) Recording of data from subjects 18 years of age or older using noninvasive procedures routinely employed in clinical practice. This includes the use of physical sensors that are applied either to the surface of the body or at a distance and do not involve input of matter or significant amounts of energy into the subject or an invasion of the subject's privacy. It also includes such procedures as weighing, testing sensory acuity, electrocardiography, electroencephalography, thermography, detection of naturally occurring radioactivity, diagnostic echography, and electroretinography. It does not include the exposure to electro-magnetic radiation outside the visible range (for example, x-rays, microwaves).

☐ 4) Collection of blood samples by venipuncture, in amounts not exceeding 450 milliliters in an eight-week period and no more often than two times per week, from subjects 18 years or older and who are in good health and not pregnant.

☐ 5) Collection of both supra- and subgingival dental plaque and calculus, provided the procedure is not more invasive than routine prophylactic scaling of the teeth and the process is accomplished in accordance with accepted prophylactic techniques.

☐ 6) Voice recordings made for research purposes such as investigation of speech defects.

☐ 7) Moderate exercise by healthy volunteers.

☐ 8) The study of existing data, documents, records, pathological specimens, or diagnostic specimens.

☐ 9) Research on individual group behavior or characteristics of individuals, such as studies of perception, cognition, game theory, or test development, where the investigator does not manipulate subjects' behavior and the research will not involve stress to subjects.

☐ 10) Research on drugs or devices for which an investigational new drug exemption or an investigational device exemption is required.

PLEASE EXPLAIN HOW YOUR PROJECT FITS INTO THE INDICATED CATEGORY IN THE "PROTOCOL" SECTION OF THIS FORM.

INSTITUTIONAL REVIEW BOARD
OFFICE OF RESEARCH & ACADEMIC DEVELOPMENT

II. ABSTRACT: (200 words or less)

III. PROTOCOL: (Describe procedures to which humans will be subjected. Use additional pages if necessary.)

IV. BENEFITS: (Describe the benefits to the individual and/or mankind.)

V. RISKS: (Describe the risks to the subject and precautions that will be taken to minimize them. Include physical, psychological and social risks.)

VI. ALTERNATIVE PROCEDURES: (Describe any alternative procedure(s) available to the subject.)

VII. CONFIDENTIALITY OF DATA: (Describe the methods to be used to ensure the confidentiality of data obtained, including plans for final disposition or destruction, debriefing procedures, etc.)

VIII. RECRUITMENT PROCEDURES: (Describe the selection of subjects and method of recruitment, including recruitment letter, if applicable.)

IX. CONSENT: (Attach a copy of the CONSENT FORM(S) to be signed by the subject and/or any STATEMENT(S) to be read to the subject, or INFORMATIONAL LETTER to be directed to the subject.)

I certify that the protocol and method of obtaining informed consent as approved by the Institutional Review Board will be followed during the period covered by this research project. Any future changes will be submitted for IRB review and approval prior to implementation.

_____   _____
Date   Project Director

HUMAN SUBJECTS REVIEW APPLIES ONLY TO THE METHOD OF USING HUMAN SUBJECTS IN RESEARCH.

INSTITUTIONAL REVIEW BOARD
OFFICE OF RESEARCH & ACADEMIC DEVELOPMENT

INSTITUTIONAL REVIEW BOARD
OFFICE OF RESEARCH & ACADEMIC DEVELOPMENT

137

CONSENT FORM CHECKLIST

N/A	YES	NO	
___	___	___	1. Is the consent form written in **"lay language"**?
___	___	___	2. Is it **free of any exculpatory language** through which the subject is made to waive any legal rights, including any release of the investigator, the sponsor, the institution or its agents from liability for negligence?
___	___	___	3. If blood is to be withdrawn, is the **standard blood withdrawal information** included: number of times; period of time covered; potential hazards, including "a bruise at the site of vein puncture, inflammation of the vein and infection," and information that "care will be taken to avoid these complications"? Use of the **Standard Blood Withdrawal Consent Form** fulfills this requirement.
___	___	___	4. If **pregnant women** are to be included as subjects, is provision made for using the required **Auditor Witness**[1] to the consent procedure?
___	___	___	5. If **children** are to be included as subjects, is provision made for securing the **assent** of the child and the **consent** of the parent(s) or guardian(s)?
___	___	___	6. **If investigational drugs or devices** are to be used, or if approved drugs or devices are to be used in a manner for which they have not been approved, are such drugs or devices identified as "experimental"?

7. Does the consent form include each of the following **basic elements of informed consent**?

N/A	YES	NO	
___	___	___	a. A statement that the study involves **research,** an explanation of the **purposes** of the research and the **expected duration** of the subject's participation.
___	___	___	b. A **description of the procedures** to be followed, and identification of any **procedures that are experimental.**
___	___	___	c. A description of any **benefits** to the subject or to others.
___	___	___	d. A description of any reasonably foreseeable **risks or discomforts.**
___	___	___	e. A disclosure of appropriate **alternative procedures** that might be advantageous to the subject.
___	___	___	f. A statement describing the extent to which **confidentiality** of records identifying the subject will be maintained.
___	___	___	g. In the case of research involving **FDA regulated products,** information that FDA and the study sponsor may inspect records identifying subjects.
___	___	___	h. For research involving **more than minimal risk,** the appropriate **"compensation statement."**[2]
___	___	___	i. An explanation of whom to contact for **answers to pertinent questions** involving the research and research subject's rights, and whom to contact in the event of a research-related injury to the subject.
___	___	___	j. A statement that participation is **voluntary,** refusal to participate will involve **no penalty or loss of benefits,** and the subject may **discontinue participation at any time without penalty or loss of benefits.**

If there was a "NO" response to any of the above questions, the consent form must be revised accordingly unless the investigator can satisfactorily justify why it is appropriate as submitted.

If the required revisions **are minor,** please indicate them on the back of this consent form for the office to retype and send to the investigator for endorsement. If the needed revisions are **extensive,** it will be the director's responsibility to make the changes and submit a copy of the resulting revised consent form.

IRB APPROVAL CANNOT BE GRANTED UNTIL A COPY OF THE APPROVED CONSENT FORM IS ON FILE IN THE OFFICE OF RESEARCH & ACADEMIC DEVELOPMENT.

[1] Auditor Witness—Someone who is present during consent procedure and signs as witness.

[2] If someone agrees to participate even though there is more than minimal risk specify what type of compensation (e.g. free treatment, hospitalization, etc.), if any, will be available.

Rochester, Michigan

Institutional Review Board
Office of Research & Academic Development

BIOSAFETY REVIEW

If a research project involves the use of recombinant DNA molecules, the research protocol must be reviewed and approved by the Institutional Biosafety Committee (IBC). This committee concerns itself with the safe use and disposal of recombinant DNA. The basic guidelines for research using recombinant DNA molecules were developed by DHS and printed in the *Federal Register* (May 7, 1986). The guidelines emphasize that it is the responsibility of the institution to adhere to the intent of the guidelines as well as to the specifics.

The institutional biosafety committee has to be made up of at least five individuals who have expertise in recombinant DNA technology, biological safety, and physical containment. Two members shall not be affiliated with the institution and are appointed to represent the interest of the community.

The IBC reviews research protocols to assess the safety of recombinant DNA experiments and any potential risk to public health or the environment. All principal investigators proposing to work with recombinant DNA molecules must provide proof of ability to work with the substance without creating a harmful situation in the research laboratory or endangering the environment.

Institutions must appoint a biological safety officer (BSO) if they engage in recombinant DNA research at the BL3 or BL4 containment level. The BSO is a member of the IBC with specific responsibilities: reporting problems, developing emergency plans, and providing technical advice.

The biosafety review committee considers whether laboratory personnel have received adequate training, whether hazardous materials will be handled properly and whether the facilities are adequate to support the proposed project. In addition to judging the proper use of hazardous materials, the IBC also determines that the method of disposal is safe for the environment. The chair of this committee is often a faculty member with expertise in handling and disposing of hazardous substances.

RADIATION SAFETY REVIEW

Colleges or universities that have research projects using radioisotopes must have a license from the Nuclear Regulatory Commission. The license lists the names of every researcher at the institution who is eligible to use radioactive materials in research, specifies the kind and amount of isotopes that can be used, and describes the accepted methods of disposal.

To initiate a research project using radioactive materials, a researcher must submit an application to the Radiation Safety Committee of the institution and be added to the existing license. Investigators who are not listed as radioisotope users on the existing license cannot submit a proposal using radioactive materials.

If an institution does not have a license, it must apply to the Nuclear Regulatory Commission for one. The license requires a quarterly review of all materials used to ensure that the institution stays within the guidelines. All proposed research projects are still reviewed by the radiation safety committee to ensure that the research protocol is within the guidelines specified by the institution's license.

The research administration office is responsible for ensuring that all research projects using radioisotopes receive approval. The institution also must appoint a radiation safety officer, who receives and distributes all radioactive materials to the individual research laboratories, updates the license regularly, and prepares for inspections from the Nuclear Regulatory Commission.

MISCONDUCT REVIEW

Misconduct review is the newest review procedure required by the PHS to ensure ethical research procedures and reporting. The specific guidelines for this are in the NIH *Guide for Grants and Contracts* (Vol. 15, No. 11).

Misconduct is defined as serious deviation—such as fabrication, falsification, or plagiarism—from accepted practices in carrying out research or in reporting the results of research. In addition, the failure to comply with federal requirements affecting specific aspects of the conduct of research, as discussed in this chapter, may also be considered misconduct. Although there had always been some instances of misconduct in research, the incidences had not been frequent enough to warrant formal policies and procedures for dealing with misconduct. But recently there seems to have been an increase either in misconduct or in the allegations of misconduct. The PHS has determined that formal policies are necessary to ensure equities and to protect the scientific community.

The other procedures described in this chapter require that a review take place before submitting a research proposal. Since misconduct in research is only an issue after the research is under way, no prior review is required. However, institutions are required to assure the PHS that they have policies and procedures for conducting an inquiry into any allegation of misconduct and that, when warranted, a full-scale investigation of the alleged misconduct will be conducted. Inquiries should be completed in no more than 30 days, and if an investigation is required, the institution is expected to complete it within 120 days. A report of the findings must then be prepared. Notification to NIH or DHS is not required when an inquiry begins; however, if an investigation is considered necessary, the NIH program officer must be informed before it begins. The name of the person involved may then be added to the PHS alert file. The PHS alert file includes information from NIH and other PHS agencies.

SUMMARY

The university research office is responsible for ensuring that the university complies with all federal, state, and local statutes and federal agency requirements on research projects. Although the principal investigator has primary responsibility for conducting his/her research according to legal and ethical guidelines, the research administration office must make sure that investigators are aware of applicable statutes and regulations.

Proposal Sign-Off Procedures

Proposal sign-off is an area of major importance to funding sources. In fact, grant applications often have explicit instructions on who must sign the proposal and how many copies must have original signatures. Unfortunately, administrators find this area problematic because many proposal developers wait until the last minute to prepare proposals and procure appropriate signatures. This procrastination results in major difficulties when the individuals with the necessary signatures are out of the office, at out-of-town meetings, or on vacation. It is my belief that the last-minute, rush-rush, sign now–read later proposals are exactly the ones that deserve a closer look.

While you may think that everyone has a sign-off procedure and an organized system that records and monitors grant proposals, this is not the case. Several of my clients who have requested grants-process audits could not tell me how many proposals their organization had submitted over the past year or the status of the submitted proposals (e.g., pending action, awarded, rejected). And in some cases, copies of proposals that had been submitted were incomplete or missing from files. In addition, many organizations have entrepreneurial grant seekers who purposely circumvent the grants office and even the requirement of signatures. If they are successful in attracting the interest of the funders, these entrepreneurs seek the necessary signatures only after the proposal has been funded.

Without a mandatory sign-off procedure, it is difficult to document the progress of the grants office and track and retrieve important data such as matching funds, commitments on submitted proposals, space allocation, and time allocation of key staff. Organizations without formal systems to record and monitor such data often find themselves being asked to explain such things as how 130 percent of a principal investigator's time could be allocated to grants.

The sign-off system differs greatly from organization to organization. The following suggestions may assist you in developing your own sign-off system and form.

The appropriate administrators, as well as those individuals who will be affected by the project, should be included in the final sign-off. Also include copies of the preproposal review forms with the final sign-off sheet to remind the signing parties of the initial conditions, concerns, and stipulations that the proposal developer/writer had to meet before gaining the individual's and organization's support. You may want to ask the proposal developer to include individual notes indicating where the necessary changes were made. This will speed up the signing process considerably.

Another method that expedites the sign-off process is the use of paper clips whose colors correspond to the areas that must be signed by each individual. Include each individual's color clip on a copy of his or her preproposal review form for easy identification. Do not allow proposal developers to ask individuals to complete preproposal review forms at the same time that they are signing off. This encourages the rush-rush approach and defeats the whole purpose of an organized sign-off system.

The rules for sign-off should be outlined in a cover sheet attached to your sign-off form. They may consist of:

- who is to sign

- when and where to sign

- how much time the individual has to review the proposal

- what the protocol is when signature is impossible owing to problems with the proposal

- where to go with questions

- how the proposal should be moved to the next appropriate individual for signature

The following section summarizes suggested procedures for moving the proposal through the system.

Maintain a numerical log of all proposals. Place the proposal by number on a piece of magnetic tape on a bulletin board. On one side of the magnetic bulletin board, place the names of the individuals required to sign off. Move the proposal identification strips from individual to individual as they sign off.

Earmark those proposals that must be expedited by a colored flag. Depending on time constraints, it may be necessary to designate an individual to be on call to move the signed proposal to the next administrator required to sign. When time is of the essence, nothing can be more upsetting than a required administrator who signs the proposal and places it in interoffice mail, resulting in a missed deadline. While your grants system may denounce the practice of submitting proposals at the last minute, the grants office should efficiently track every proposal through the sign-off procedure, whether it be of the rush-rush type or one being submitted early.

Many nonprofit organizations now have board presidents, as well as administrators, sign off on proposals. Although the funder may not require board sign-off, it is a good idea, since board members are legally responsible for the organization's actions. In addition, this extra sign-off can demonstrate board knowledge and commitment to your project—one thing that your competition may fail to show.

Recording and Monitoring Matching Funds

The Preproposal Review Form provides a space to record possible matching-funds needs. By the time the final sign-off form is ready to be circulated, information concerning the funding source's requirements for matching or in-kind contributions should be known. The final sign-off form should include information on the matching funds that must be committed to a project if it gets funded, and the grants-office administrator should provide this information to the individual responsible for the organization's commitment.

Of greater significance is the documentation and monitoring of this commitment so that any possible audits will support the contribution. In-kind contributions of personnel services and space, as well as matching money, can best be recorded in the grants office, since it has the greatest knowledge of the funding source and its requirements. (Your grants office should have an Office of Management and Budget circular that outlines the federal guidelines for the documentation of matching funds.)

A grants office that knows its success rate can more easily predict its matching funds' needs. However, even with this information, predicting the exact requirements for matching funds can be difficult because not all grants call for matching contributions. Organized nonprofit groups allocate matching funds and in-kind resources by organizational priorities and mission and the grants office's plan. Each grant-seeking priority is allocated a certain amount of matching funds. In addition, some organizations allocate a specific amount for staff interests. Organizations also often allow for a contingency fund, to be used in the event that the overall grants success rate is greater than anticipated.

Priority areas and their matching-funds budget should always be documented on Preproposal Review Forms and sign-off sheets so that the appropriate administrators have the necessary information to make allocation decisions. To help you in this area, a Matching Funds Checklist and Matching Funds Worksheet appear at the end of this section.

Submission and Follow-Up with Funding Sources

The grants administration office should be the *only* office that submits proposals to outside funding sources. This will ensure that all proposals receive the proper internal sign-off as well as meet all of the funding source's requirements. Many of the grants office's functions can be accomplished only if it is mandatory that submission occurs only through the office.

PROPOSAL IDENTIFICATION NUMBER

Unfortunately, many organizations do not affix an internal identification or logging number to a proposal until after final sign-off procedures have been carried out and submittal is virtually assured. Since one function of the grants office is the generation of data relevant to the grants effort and the mission of the organization, it is necessary to keep a record of:

- who is initiating proposals
- the funding sources approached
- pending grants
- the proposal success rate (funded proposals vs. submitted proposals)

MATCHING FUNDS CHECKLIST

1. Do you have a definite matching funds allocation/budget?

2. Are matching funds allocated by an established priority?

3. Are all commitments for matching funds listed on preproposal review forms and/or sign-off sheets?

4. Are all matching funds commitments recorded by the grants office?

5. Can the grants office provide a running tally of matching funds commitments within minutes?

MATCHING FUNDS WORKSHEET

1. Total amount of matching funds available $ _____

2. Matching funds already allocated to accepted proposals:

Proposal _____   Amount $ _____

_____ $ _____

_____ $ _____

_____ $ _____

_____ $ _____

Subtotal $ _____

3. Remaining matching funds available $ _____
(#1 minus subtotal of #2)

4. Matching funds in pending proposals:

Pending
Proposal _____   Amount $ _____

_____ $ _____

_____ $ _____

_____ $ _____

_____ $ _____

Subtotal $ _____

5. Estimate of success rate of pending proposals (%) _____

6. Estimate of matching funds needed for pending proposals $ _____
(Apply percentage #5 to subtotal of #4)

Notes: _____

_____

_____

_____

_____

_____

_____

_____

_____

_____

A number identification system can supply this information plus other valuable information that can quickly designate the researcher and department or division. Early identification of the proposal idea can provide data on who follows through on proposal preparation and uses the investment of the grants office in preproposal activity. An identification number on a proposal idea will help track the developing proposal through the organization. And since a proposal idea may have more than one title and may be referred to in different ways and with various abbreviations, an identification number can help avoid confusion.

To develop your identification system, review your past submittals to determine which funding sources were sent the greatest number of your proposals. Arrange your identification numbers according to the most frequently used funding sources.

Sample Identification Systems (First Three Digits)

001–009   Federal Funding Sources
    001–020 = Education Programs
    021–030 = Department of Defense
    031–040 = National Science Foundation
    041–050 = National Endowment for the Arts

100–199   Private Foundations
    100–120 = National General Purpose
    121–130 = Special-Interest Health
    131–140 = Special-Interest Higher Education

200–299   Corporations
    200–220 = Light-Electronics Firms
    221–230 = Medical Supplies

300–399   State Funding Sources
    300–320 = State Department of Transportation

The number of categories can be expanded and divided so that you can determine if the proposal award is a contract or grant, and letters can be added for greater identification. For example, a grantee may use the following letter code to designate the size of the proposal award.

    A = over $500,000
    B = $250,000–$499,999
    C = $100,000–$249,999
    D = $25,000–$ 99,999
    E = $ 5,000–$ 24,999
    F = under $4,999

Letters can designate departments in your organization and even the researcher or project director. For example, 201-FS-8/1 is a proposal submitted to a light-electronics firm. *F* indicates that the proposal request was less than $5,000. *S* designates your organization's investigator, department, or division. The *8* of the 8/1 indicates the year (1988), and the *1* indicates that it was the first proposal submitted in 1988.

A numbering system also helps you keep accurate files, which will prove beneficial should the funding source call you and refer to a proposal. While you are looking for it, you can at least sound intelligent, since the system will allow you to identify the approximate dollar amount of the proposal, the grant writer, the area of interest that it addresses, and the department that submitted it.

Other variables that are important to your organization may also be included in your identification system. For example:

- the number of years a proposal is funded for

- the type of reimbursement system that will be used (e.g., cost reimbursement, cash advance)

- specific requests of the funding source (e.g., secrecy, confidentiality)

- a possible patent-rights coding that may serve to remind all staff to place the proposal back in a locked file, etc.

In addition to statistical and record-keeping functions, the identification system will help track the progress of proposals through your organization. You might use your computer to provide daily or weekly updates of each proposal's stage of development.

Another effective way to easily identify and track developing proposals is to use washable, magnetic bulletin boards and reusable magnetic plastic strips. The grant I.D. number and other pertinent information can be listed on the special material that sticks to the magnetic bulletin board. As a grant moves through the stages of development, sign-off, submittal, and eventual award or denial, the magnetic strip can be moved and information added easily (funding-source logging numbers, etc.). The use of colored magnetic materials can let you see the necessary components or restrictions of any one proposal at a glance.

In summary, your identification system should do more for you and your organization than just put your proposal submittals in chronological order. To give you an idea of what the system can do, see the Checklist for Submission and Follow-up Procedures.

CHECKLIST FOR SUBMISSION
AND FOLLOW-UP PROCEDURES

1. Does your grants office have final sign-off and overall control of the sub-mission procedure?

2. Is there a system in place to identify proposals in their various stages of development?

3. Is there a tracking system that allows you to follow and identify where proposals are at all times?

4. If you have a numbering system, does it allow you to know who wrote the proposal, what kind of funding source the proposal was sent to, how much the request was for, and when the proposal was submitted?

SUBMISSION TO PUBLIC FUNDING SOURCES

Submission of proposals to public funding sources requires a much different and more complex procedure than submission to private funding sources. Because you are dealing with public funds, procedures for submittal and deadlines must comply with public-information laws and give equal notice and opportunity to everyone.

Government officials cannot grant any leeway on deadlines. Proposal deadlines for federal programs are published in the Federal Register. A change in a deadline must be announced in the register thirty days in advance to allow ample time for all grant seekers to adjust to the new deadline date.

Whether your grants system is proactive (proposal development is initiated months before the deadline date) or reactive (proposal development is initiated a few hours before the deadline), the federal rules are clear and unyielding. Once the required signatures have been affixed to the proposal, it follows a definite system.

Read your guidelines carefully. Some government programs require a preapplication that, among other things, determines applicant eligibility. If this step is required, be sure to include all references to your approved eligibility when submitting the full proposal.

The federal government has made state review of federal grants to nonprofit organizations an option of each state. Some states may require this intergovernmental review process; however, local and state review of all federal programs is not necessary. Executive Order 12372 says that a state must require that federally funded proposed projects be reviewed by appropriate local and state officials if they are potentially at cross-purposes to programs and priorities at the local and state levels.

To make sure that your proposal does not fall under your state's elective review, contact your governor's office or the federal agency you are applying to, or check the Federal Register that published the grant's rules and regulations for the program in question. Once you locate the state office that is responsible for the checking procedure (called your "state single point of contact"), discuss the situation with a representative of the office to avoid any conflict. If your state requires a review, submit your proposal and your application to the funding source at the same time. Your state's review and comments will be submitted to the federal agency within sixty days.

The federal agency must either address the concerns outlined in your state's comments and follow the recommendations made or explain why it chose not to. The federal agency is not bound by the state's recommendation, and funds can be granted as the agency sees fit.

Follow all federal instructions carefully to ensure that your proposal is accurately addressed, labeled, and mailed. If you are delivering the proposal by hand or by messenger, be sure to check that it reaches the proper point. Federal programs use proposal-logging centers. Many federal proposal packages contain a return card that is completed and mailed back to you. This means that your proposal reached the logging center but does not necessarily mean it has been delivered by the logging center to the appropriate funding program.

While your proposal usually makes it from the logging center to the appropriate program, a follow-up call may be in order, and it is a necessity if you have not received a return card.

Most federal guidelines call for your proposal to be postmarked at a United States postal office before a certain date. Retain your receipt in case your proposal does not get to the appropriate program officer. A postmarked receipt will prove that your proposal has been lost and allow you to resubmit a copy.

SUBMISSION TO PRIVATE FUNDING SOURCES

An organization appears to be a poor steward of funds if it does not comply with deadlines. Therefore, be prompt when you submit your proposal. Find out if early submission will give you favorable treatment and how many copies of the proposal the funding source would like. Applications frequently instruct you to submit one or two copies when the funding source could actually use five.

The submittal process for private funding sources is not subject to the rules that govern federal agencies. Private funders have a variety of deadlines and frequently experience a time lag between submittal date and evaluation by staff and/or board members. Thus, failure to adhere to an exact deadline does not necessarily mean that your proposal will not be considered or will automatically be placed in the next funding cycle.

Follow the mailing instructions provided by the funder. Many funders enforce a strict length requirement for proposals, so be wary of placing a cover letter over your letter proposal. Record the submittal date of your proposal, and retain your postal receipt.

The following suggestions on how to submit proposals to private funders may be helpful to your grants office.

- Send the contacts uncovered through your webbing and linkage system an abstract of the proposal or a copy of the letter proposal.

- Ask friends of the funding source to push for your proposal at the board meeting.

- Ask friends of the funding source to use their contacts to try for a favorable decision.

- Minimize personal contact with the funding source once you have submitted the proposal.

- When it comes time to submit your request, consider delivering it in person if you are located near the funding source, or use an advocate or board member to deliver it for you. Hand delivery makes more of an impression on funding agencies, and it also helps you avoid problems with the postal service.

THE GRANTS OFFICE'S ROLE IN RESPONDING TO THE FUNDER'S DECISION

The worksheets and checklists in the following sections are designed for the grants administrator to review and include as part of the grants-office procedures manual.

The grants office is the official sender of the proposal, but the funder may call or write to the individual listed as project director for questions or budget negotiations. While the grants office's goal is usually to encourage the grant writer to assume responsibility for the proposal, it's crucial for the office to know when the funder makes contact with your organization.

The funding source may also contact the project director to arrange a site visit to your organization. This visit requires special planning. What materials will be presented and who will present them and represent the organization must be predetermined. The plans for the visit should be coordinated through one office, and the grants office may be the logical choice.

If the funding source requests more information, the request should be channeled through the grants office, or the complete grant file will miss changes and modifications. Once the transmission of important data begins to by-pass the grants office, the potential for embarrassing mistakes builds.

DEALING WITH THE DECISION OF THE PUBLIC FUNDING SOURCE

You will receive a response to your proposal several months after its submittal. The response will be:

- accepted

- accepted with budget modifications (i.e., let's talk about the budget)

- approved but not funded

- supportable but not fundable

- rejected

Monitoring contact with funders becomes even more important when dealing with the decision on the proposal. To ensure that your organization's image will be upheld throughout this critical phase, only one office must be responsible for handling contact with the federal funding source.

Review the suggestions outlined under each possible response to your proposal in the Public Funding Decision Checklist. Identify those suggestions that are *now* part of your grants-office procedures and determine who is currently responsible for each of them. Then select which of the remaining suggestions will be added to your existing procedures. Note, however, that you should always request a list of the successful grantees and a description of the reviewers irrespective of the funding decision.

FOLLOW-UP WITH PUBLIC FUNDING SOURCES

The funding source should view follow-up as an asset rather than a nuisance. Your follow-up activities should position you as an asset in your field of interest, not a pest.

The following Public Funding Source Follow-up Checklist contains suggestions on how to get to know a funding source better and how to maintain a good relationship. Review this list and determine which suggestions are currently being implemented by members of your organization and which ones should be implemented in the future. If you do not currently do so, be sure to disseminate a list of follow-up suggestions to all of the successful and unsuccessful grantees in your organization.

PUBLIC FUNDING DECISION CHECKLIST

Two blanks correspond to each suggestion listed. Check the first box if the suggestion is *currently* one of your grants-office procedures. Check the second box if it is *not currently* a procedure but is one which you would like to incorporate in the *future*. At the end of each suggestion, indicate who is now responsible for implementing the suggestion or who will be responsible in the future.

Accepted

__ __ 1. Send a thank-you letter.

__ __ 2. Request a critique of your proposal to learn what the funding source liked about it.

__ __ 3. Ask the funding source to visit you or set up a visit to them.

__ __ 4. Request any completion forms to learn what records you need to keep.

__ __ 5. Ask the funding source what are common problems with grants like yours and how to avoid them.

Accepted with Budget Modifications

__ __ 1. Send a thank-you letter.

__ __ 2. The funding source will probably call you. When they do, refer them to your project planner to negotiate the budget items.

__ __ 3. Select the methods you would consider eliminating, and isolate the associated costs.

__ __ 4. Reduce the amount of change predicted in the objectives or the number of people to be served by the project.

__ __ 5. Be prepared to turn down the funds before you enter into an agreement that will cause you to lose your credibility later.

Approved but Not Funded

— — 1. Send a thank-you letter.

— — 2. Call the funding source and ask them how far from the funding cut-off point you were.

— — 3. Ask what you could have done better.

— — 4. Request the reviewers' comments.

— — 5. Try to get additional appropriations. Remember that federal bureaucrats get their funds from appropriations, and anything you can do to increase those funds will earn you great respect by funding sources. Additional funds may mean a better chance of getting your proposal funded.

— — 6. Ask if there are any discretionary funds left over for unsolicited proposals.

Rejected

— — 1. Send a thank-you letter.

— — 2. Request the reviewers' comments (enclose a self-addressed stamped envelope for convenience).

— — 3. Ask the funding official for his or her suggestions.

— — 4. Ask if the proposal could be funded as a pilot project, needs-assessment study, or some other way.

— — 5. Ask if there are any ways the funding source could assist you in getting ready for the next submission.

— — 6. Ask what your chances are if you try again and what you would have to change to increase your chances of success.

— — 7. Ask if you could become a reviewer to learn and become more familiar with the review process.

PUBLIC FUNDING SOURCE FOLLOW-UP CHECKLIST

1. Send the funding source notes on special articles or books in your area or field.

2. Invite the funding source to visit you.

3. Ask the funding source to review an article you are writing.

4. Ask the funding source to speak at a conference or seminar, particularly a special grants conference.

5. Ask the funding source what you could do to have an impact on legislation affecting their agency.

6. Watch for meetings announced in the Federal Register and testify at committee hearings that have impact on the agency and its funding level.

7. Send the agency blind carbon copies of your efforts to have an impact on legislation for them (and yourself).

8. Use your association memberships and legislative committees to write and push for changes that benefit the particular agency.

9. Remain on the funding source's mailing list, and review the Federal Register for upcoming opportunities with the funding source.

10. Visit the funding source personally.

Remember, do not wait until next year's deadline to begin thinking about your application—start right after the decision. The aggressive grant seeker does not shelve the project for eleven months. The best way to know what is going on with the funding source is to keep in contact!

DEALING WITH THE DECISION OF THE PRIVATE FUNDING SOURCE

Private funding sources generally make their decision and let you know the outcome promptly. You will get a simple yes (accepted) or no (rejected). If the funding source says your proposal is "supportable" but "not fundable," it is a polite no. The easiest way to tell if your grant is funded is by looking for the check.

Review the following suggestions outlined in the Private Funding Decision Checklist. If the response is yes—the grant seeker's dream—do the suggestions *immediately.* If it is no—the dreaded response—turn it into a yes for next year by following the suggestions.

FOLLOW-UP WITH PRIVATE FUNDING SOURCES

Keeping your contacts current is the best way to continue success with private funding sources. A system of informing the funders of your activities both by mail and in person is optimum.

Once they have given away their money, many funding sources feel neglected by grantees. You can get on a funding source's list of good grantees through follow-up. See the following Private Funding Source Follow-up Checklist for suggestions.

PRIVATE FUNDING DECISION CHECKLIST

Two boxes correspond to each suggestion listed. Check the first box if the suggestion is currently one of your grants-office procedures. Check the second box if it is not currently a procedure but is one which you would like to incorporate in the future. At the end of each suggestion, indicate who is now responsible, or should be in the future, for implementing the suggestion.

Current	Future	ACCEPTED (YES)
		1. Send a thank-you letter. (A foundation reported funding 10% of the proposals submitted to it and receiving very few thank-you letters. An official from the foundation said the funding results created "one ingrate and nine angry, rejected grantees.")
		2. Find out the payment procedures.
		3. Check on any reporting procedures the funding source may have.
		4. Ask the funding source for an on-site visit or a visit by you to them to report on the grant.
		5. Put the funding source on your public relations list so you can send them news releases about you.
		6. IMPORTANT: Ask the funding source for their comments or critique of your proposal. Ask them what they liked and what could have been improved.

		REJECTED (NO)
		1. Send a thank-you letter. Express your appreciation for the time and effort spent reviewing your proposal.
		2. Remind them of your need of them as a source of funds.
		3. Ask them for comments on your proposal.
		4. Ask if they would look favorably on resubmission with certain changes.
		5. Ask them if they know of any other funding source that would be interested in your project.

PRIVATE FUNDING SOURCE
FOLLOW-UP CHECKLIST

1. Put the funding source on your public relations list, and send them news releases on your agency, organization, program, etc.

2. Send the funding source articles or studies related to your area of concern.

3. Invite the funding source to visit you.

4. Keep your funding-source files updated. Have a staff member or volunteer periodically add lists of new grants awarded to the files.

5. Let the funding source know how successful you are two years after your funding. Commend them for their farsightedness in dealing with the problem, etc.

6. Send thank-you letters to funding sources for both awarded *and* rejected proposals.

GRANTS OFFICE INVENTORY
Chapter 8
The Role of the Grants Office in Assurances, Submission and Follow-Up

For Each Activity/Item Listed, Check Status:

Activity/Item	Reviewed, Appropriate Part of Grants Office	Reviewed, Appropriate Part of Other Office (List)	Reviewed, Not Applicable	Reviewed, Inappropriate Needs Action	Non-existent, Needs Action
1. Assurances • checklist of assurances for each type of funding source and policy for sign-off on assurances as they are met • policy for informing individuals and offices of their particular responsibilities in deal-					

Complete this Section for Each Activity/Item Needing Action:

What Needs to Be Accomplished? (Activity/Item)	By Whom? (Office/Person)	By When? (Time Frame)	Resources, Required—Personnel, Supplies, Equipment, Programming, etc.	Estimated Costs

GRANTS OFFICE INVENTORY
Chapter 8 *(continued)*
The Role of the Grants Office in Assurances, Submission and Follow-Up

For Each Activity/Item Listed, Check Status:

Activity/Item	Reviewed, Appropriate Part of Grants Office	Reviewed, Appropriate Part of Other Office (List)	Reviewed, Not Applicable	Reviewed, Inappropriate Needs Action	Non-existent, Needs Action
ing with the funder's restrictions 2. Internal review • form available to track internal review • central file listing all commitments 3. Animal research • approved assurance statement					

Complete this Section for Each Activity/Item Needing Action:

What Needs to Be Accomplished? (Activity/Item)	By Whom? (Office/ Person)	By When? (Time Frame)	Resources, Required— Personnel, Supplies, Equipment, Programming, etc.	Estimated Costs

GRANTS OFFICE INVENTORY

Chapter 8 *(continued)*

The Role of the Grants Office in Assurances, Submission and Follow-Up

For Each Activity/Item Listed, Check Status:

Activity/Item	Reviewed, Appropriate Part of Grants Office	Reviewed, Appropriate Part of Other Office (List)	Reviewed, Not Applicable	Reviewed, Inappropriate Needs Action	Non-existent, Needs Action
• IACUC composition requirements • notice of intent form available to investigators • copies of guidebook available to investigators 4. Human subjects research • human subjects					

Complete this Section for Each Activity/Item Needing Action:

What Needs to Be Accomplished? (Activity/Item)	By Whom? (Office/Person)	By When? (Time Frame)	Resources, Required—Personnel, Supplies, Equipment, Programming, etc.	Estimated Costs

GRANTS OFFICE INVENTORY

Chapter 8 *(continued)*

The Role of the Grants Office in Assurances, Submission and Follow-Up

For Each Activity/Item Listed, Check Status:

Activity/Item	Reviewed, Appropriate Part of Grants Office	Reviewed, Appropriate Part of Other Office (List)	Reviewed, Not Applicable	Reviewed, Inappropriate Needs Action	Non-existent, Needs Action
assurance on file • IRB committee composition meets guidelines • consent forms meet guideline requirements • human subjects review form available to investigators • guidelines available to investigators					

Complete this Section for Each Activity/Item Needing Action:

What Needs to Be Accomplished? (Activity/Item)	By Whom? (Office/Person)	By When? (Time Frame)	Resources, Required—Personnel, Supplies, Equipment, Programming, etc.	Estimated Costs

GRANTS OFFICE INVENTORY

Chapter 8 *(continued)*

The Role of the Grants Office in Assurances, Submission and Follow-Up

For Each Activity/Item Listed, Check Status:

Activity/Item	Reviewed, Appropriate Part of Grants Office	Reviewed, Appropriate Part of Other Office (List)	Reviewed, Not Applicable	Reviewed, Inappropriate Needs Action	Non-existent, Needs Action
5. Biosafety committee • IBC composition meets requirements • biological safety officer • regulations available to investigators 6. Radiation safety • review committee composition meets requirements					

Complete this Section for Each Activity/Item Needing Action:

What Needs to Be Accomplished? (Activity/Item)	By Whom? (Office/Person)	By When? (Time Frame)	Resources, Required—Personnel, Supplies, Equipment, Programming, etc.	Estimated Costs

GRANTS OFFICE INVENTORY

Chapter 8 *(continued)*

The Role of the Grants Office in Assurances, Submission and Follow-Up

For Each Activity/Item Listed, Check Status:

Activity/Item	Reviewed, Appropriate Part of Grants Office	Reviewed, Appropriate Part of Other Office (List)	Reviewed, Not Applicable	Reviewed, Inappropriate Needs Action	Non-existent, Needs Action
• appointed radiation safety officer • up-to-date license • regulations available to investigators 7. Misconduct in research • procedure for inquiry • procedure for investigation					

Complete this Section for Each Activity/Item Needing Action:

What Needs to Be Accomplished? (Activity/Item)	By Whom? (Office/Person)	By When? (Time Frame)	Resources, Required— Personnel, Supplies, Equipment, Programming, etc.	Estimated Costs

GRANTS OFFICE INVENTORY

Chapter 8 *(continued)*

The Role of the Grants Office in Assurances, Submission and Follow-Up

For Each Activity/Item Listed, Check Status:

Activity/Item	Reviewed, Appropriate Part of Grants Office	Reviewed, Appropriate Part of Other Office (List)	Reviewed, Not Applicable	Reviewed, Inappropriate Needs Action	Non-existent, Needs Action
8. Proposal sign-off procedures • rules, forms, etc. for sign-off • system for recording & monitoring grant proposals 9. System for recording and monitoring matching funds and in-kind contributions					

Complete this Section for Each Activity/Item Needing Action:

What Needs to Be Accomplished? (Activity/Item)	By Whom? (Office/Person)	By When? (Time Frame)	Resources, Required—Personnel, Supplies, Equipment, Programming, etc.	Estimated Costs

GRANTS OFFICE INVENTORY

Chapter 8 *(continued)*

The Role of the Grants Office in Assurances, Submission and Follow-Up

For Each Activity/Item Listed, Check Status:

Activity/Item	Reviewed, Appropriate Part of Grants Office	Reviewed, Appropriate Part of Other Office (List)	Reviewed, Not Applicable	Reviewed, Inappropriate Needs Action	Non-existent, Needs Action
• documentation of priority areas in relationship to matching funds' budget 10. Submission and follow-up • internal identification system for logging each proposal (number-identification system, tracking system, etc.)					

Complete this Section for Each Activity/Item Needing Action:

What Needs to Be Accomplished? (Activity/Item)	By Whom? (Office/Person)	By When? (Time Frame)	Resources, Required—Personnel, Supplies, Equipment, Programming, etc.	Estimated Costs

GRANTS OFFICE INVENTORY

Chapter 8 *(continued)*

The Role of the Grants Office in Assurances, Submission and Follow-Up

For Each Activity/Item Listed, Check Status:

Activity/Item	Reviewed, Appropriate Part of Grants Office	Reviewed, Appropriate Part of Other Office (List)	Reviewed, Not Applicable	Reviewed, Inappropriate Needs Action	Non-existent, Needs Action
• standardized policy and procedures for: —submission to private and public funding sources —dealing with the funding source's decision —follow-up with private and public funding sources					

Complete this Section for Each Activity/Item Needing Action:

What Needs to Be Accomplished? (Activity/Item)	By Whom? (Office/Person)	By When? (Time Frame)	Resources, Required— Personnel, Supplies, Equipment, Programming, etc.	Estimated Costs

CHAPTER 9

The Role of the Grants Office in the Administration of Private Funds

The Negotiation of the Final Budget

To ensure the fiscal integrity of the grants effort of the organization, all budget negotiations must include the grants office. Use of personal contact and conference phone calls that include representation by the grants office are strongly advised. Nonprofit organizations that allow project directors a free hand in budget negotiation are placing the proposed grant recipient in a difficult position. In the excitement of actually being awarded the grant, the project director may forget to think of the mission of the organization above self during negotiations, and he or she may be willing to reduce monies in the budget to recover institutional costs to meet the necessary cuts. Although some project directors do well in budget negotiations, others make the mistake of thinking that certain cuts are no problem. For example, they may see no difficulty in cutting costs, picking up travel and telephone costs someplace else, or providing the same project and scope of work for $20,000 less in support.

It is a problem to concede to a request for the same amount of work for less money. The funding source may feel that if you could have accomplished the same thing with $20,000 less, your original request should have been smaller. In short, you are viewed as a liar when you agree to less money without changing the scope of work.

To develop a great amount of respect for your organization, follow the trustee approach to negotiation. The grant/contract is an agreement between your organization and the funding source to accomplish tasks that you have prescribed to meet the objectives of the grant. Acting as a trustee of the grant money makes you want to be sure that the funder receives exactly what it paid for in the most cost-efficient manner possible.

The budget negotiations should center on methods and deal with deleting activities and modifying the amount of change called for in meeting the objectives. Most funding sources will discuss decreases in budget categories as if they had nothing to do with the methods/ activities. This is where your project planner will be very useful. It will remind the funder that the expectations of the grant/contract must be reduced in relationship to the reduction of funds. Accurate knowledge of expectations will help to ensure your future relationship with the funder.

Trustee is defined as one to whom another's property or management is entrusted. One has faith and confidence in a trustee. By using your project planner to negotiate, you can build this confidence and trust.

You can eliminate a method or two and still meet your objective. However, when several methods are eliminated, you must reduce the change represented in the objective, and in some instances, you may even have to eliminate the objective. Remember, the reduction of funding in any area has a direct impact on your ability to complete the activity. For example, if the project director's salary is disputed, look at the activities he or she must direct. A job description is the sum of the skills required in accomplishing the methods. Set minimum experience requirements and estimate the cost of hiring a person who meets these standards. Discussion should center not on the project director's salary, or any other personnel costs, but on the qualifications needed to accomplish the prescribed tasks. Of course, you could lower the project director's salary by hiring someone with less credentials and experience, but while this individual might cost less initially, he or she would take longer to accomplish tasks. Reducing the project's nonpersonnel budget items will also affect your ability to carry out activities and accomplish objectives.

Approach the final budget negotiations as if your organization and the funder were partners in the grant outcome: your proposal uses the funders money to address a mutual concern; you are a steward of the funds. Your organization's image and working relationship with the funding source will be greatly enhanced by reinforcing this cooperative attitude.

Official Acceptance

The grants office should handle the official acceptance of the grant. This includes the responsibility of notifying your organization and *initiating* public notification if applicable.

The funding source should be asked about rules or preferences concerning the publicizing of awards. The grants office is responsible for ensuring compliance with the funder's rules and regulations. The office should review any other restrictions the funder may have before the acceptance letter is signed and returned. It is a good idea to review the Official Acceptance Checklist at the end of this section.

The official acceptance letter, whether written by a high-ranking administrator or a grants-office staff member, should make reference to your grants administration staff and include their phone numbers and note the grants office's willingness to assist in the proper transfer of funds. The letter should also encourage the funder to call the grants office for any reason at all so that the office can stay on top of the funder's concerns.

Record Keeping and Reporting

A survey conducted by David G. Bauer Associates, Inc., revealed that the majority of foundations responding to questions concerning financial record-keeping requirements expected their grant recipients to abide by the guidelines established by the American Institute of Certified Public Accountants. This 5-volume guide to financial reporting is published by the Commerce Clearinghouse of Chicago and can be found in most libraries. Another good guide is *Generally Accepted Accounting Principles,* published by Harcourt, Brace, Jovanovich. However, nonprofit organizations should retain the services of a professional accountant who is familiar with these accounting standards.

Many of the twenty thousand small foundations do not have sufficient staff to audit grantee records. In any case, the grantee should do a completion report, including a statement showing income received (grant funds) and the expenditure of this income. A completion report should be submitted to the funding source even if it is not mandated. While the funder may not review this fiscal report, the fact that you submitted it may enhance your image as a true trustee of their funds.

Budget Modification

While private funding sources have different rules on budget modifications, most will allow changes in budget that do not modify the purpose or intent of the grant. Since fewer than 1,000 of the 24,859 active foundations have offices, full-time directors, and staffs, the private marketplace does not have a large bureaucracy. Private foundations simply do not have the time to develop or institute elaborate forms and rules for budget changes.

Since many foundations meet only once or twice a year and have a limited ability to respond to requests for budget changes, they are usually not concerned with reallocations within budget categories but do not want the approved grant total to be exceeded. You may even send a small foundation a letter of notice stating that you are moving budget amounts and categories as outlined unless they instruct you to the contrary within thirty days.

I once purchased the equipment called for on a foundation grant at a tremendous savings by buying it below wholesale, and as a result, my original equipment budget was left with a considerable balance. When I checked with the funding source for approval to purchase additional equipment with the money I saved, my organization was commended for being a good trustee of funds. The foundation gave us permission to use all of the remaining funds for the purchase of additional equipment related to the grant. Please note that most funders do not like grantees to return funds. This disturbs their accounting system and affects government rules concerning expenditures and IRS returns. If you are interested in modifying your budget, review the following Checklist for Budget Modification with Private Funds.

Equipment and Purchasing Controls

All equipment purchased through grants from private funders should have an inventory tag and corresponding number that is recorded in the grants office. The numbering system used should identify:

- the funding source that granted the equipment
- the location of the equipment (what department, laboratory, building, etc.)
- the investigator, project director, or manager responsible for the equipment
- any special rules, regulations, and so on related to the equipment, such as warranties, maintenance requirements, life expectancy (how many years it will be operable), and resale restrictions

Whether you put this information into a computer or have a manual filing system, it should be readily available. For example, you should be able to quickly produce pertinent lists and reports such as Outdated Equipment for Surplus.

There are few restrictions on purchase guidelines with private funders. There is usually *no* mandated policy or requirement to go out for bid on equipment. Foundations assume that you want to get the most for your money, and if you decide to purchase locally so that you receive good maintenance but pay a little more, that's your business. Before you acquire more equipment with foundation funds, take a look at the Checklist for Equipment and Purchasing Controls With Private Funds.

Cash Requests

Unlike federal funding sources, private funders generally do not require that funds be expended by the grantee and then reimbursed. Private funding sources usually operate cash-in-advance systems. The only variable is how much of the granted sum will come in advance. Many small family foundations provide grantees with lump-sum advance payments. However, most large private funding sources have a sufficient number of staff to operate partial- or installment-payment systems. Since there are few rules in this area, a frank discussion of your cash-flow needs with the funding source will most likely result in an amicable agreement. The use of your time line and project planner will be helpful in this endeavor, as will the Checklist for Cash Requests of Private Funders.

Private funds may be deposited in savings accounts. The earned interest that accrues, ethically and legally, belongs to your organization.

Personnel Requirements and Procedures

Private funders will expect you to follow the personnel procedures accepted by the American Institute of Certified Public Accountants. These standard payroll records are usually accepted for both expenditure of the grant funds and documentation of the donation of in-kind services and matching funds.

You will be expected to follow accepted standards and fair employment practices. However, you usually will not be required to sign any assurances or compliances.

OFFICIAL ACCEPTANCE CHECKLIST

1. What office or person is in charge of official acceptances?

2. Are the funder's fiscal and report procedures requested in the acceptance letter?

3. Who does the funder call with fiscal questions?

4. Who coordinates or records the contacting of advocates, politicians, and other helpers in the grants process?

CHECKLIST FOR BUDGET MODIFICATION WITH PRIVATE FUNDS

1. What office or person in your organization is responsible for obtaining and recording approval to reallocate funds disseminated from private funders?

2. Are there any guidelines for requesting changes in private funding budget allocations?

CHECKLIST FOR EQUIPMENT AND PURCHASING CONTROLS WITH PRIVATE FUNDS

1. Does your organization have an equipment-numbering system?

2. If you do have a system, what information does it hold, and is the information filed on computer or manually?

3. What person or office in your organization is responsible for maintaining the system?

CHECKLIST FOR CASH REQUESTS OF PRIVATE FUNDERS

1. Does your organization have written procedures or a policy on who negotiates with private funding sources?

2. Are certain items on each proposed budget identified in advance as "negotiable if necessary"?

3. Does someone or some office in your organization establish the funder's cash policy in advance of the award. If so, who?

GRANTS OFFICE INVENTORY
Chapter 9
The Role of the Grants Office in the Administration of Private Funds

For Each Activity/Item Listed, Check Status:

Activity/Item	Reviewed, Appropriate Part of Grants Office	Reviewed, Appropriate Part of Other Office (List)	Reviewed, Not Applicable	Reviewed, Inappropriate Needs Action	Non-existent, Needs Action
1. Budget negotiations • designation of person or office to handle all budget negotiations • policies and procedures on how to negotiate budgets —center around methods, deleting activities, and modifying amount of change					

Complete this Section for Each Activity/Item Needing Action:

What Needs to Be Accomplished? (Activity/Item)	By Whom? (Office/Person)	By When? (Time Frame)	Resources, Required— Personnel, Supplies, Equipment, Programming, etc.	Estimated Costs

GRANTS OFFICE INVENTORY

Chapter 9 *(continued)*

The Role of the Grants Office in the Administration of Private Funds

For Each Activity/Item Listed, Check Status:

Activity/Item	Reviewed, Appropriate Part of Grants Office	Reviewed, Appropriate Part of Other Office (List)	Reviewed, Not Applicable	Reviewed, Inappropriate Needs Action	Non-existent, Needs Action
—"negotiable items if necessary" identified prior to discussions 2. Official acceptance • designation of person or office in charge of official acceptance • system to ensure that funding source restrictions are reviewed prior to signature and sub-					

Complete this Section for Each Activity/Item Needing Action:

What Needs to Be Accomplished? (Activity/Item)	By Whom? (Office/Person)	By When? (Time Frame)	Resources, Required—Personnel, Supplies, Equipment, Programming, etc.	Estimated Costs

GRANTS OFFICE INVENTORY

Chapter 9 *(continued)*

The Role of the Grants Office in the Administration of Private Funds

For Each Activity/Item Listed, Check Status:

Activity/Item	Reviewed, Appropriate Part of Grants Office	Reviewed, Appropriate Part of Other Office (List)	Reviewed, Not Applicable	Reviewed, Inappropriate Needs Action	Non-existent, Needs Action
mittal of acceptance letter • guidelines for what should be included in the acceptance letter 3. Record keeping and reporting • designation of person or office in charge of record keeping and reporting					

Complete this Section for Each Activity/Item Needing Action:

What Needs to Be Accomplished? (Activity/Item)	By Whom? (Office/ Person)	By When? (Time Frame)	Resources, Required— Personnel, Supplies, Equipment, Programming, etc.	Estimated Costs

GRANTS OFFICE INVENTORY
Chapter 9 *(continued)*
The Role of the Grants Office in the Administration of Private Funds

For Each Activity/Item Listed, Check Status:

Activity/Item	Reviewed, Appropriate Part of Grants Office	Reviewed, Appropriate Part of Other Office (List)	Reviewed, Not Applicable	Reviewed, Inappropriate Needs Action	Non-existent, Needs Action
• availability of financial reporting guidelines established by American Institute of Certified Public Accountants • retainment of services of professional accountant • submission of completion report to all private funding sources					

Complete this Section for Each Activity/Item Needing Action:

What Needs to Be Accomplished? (Activity/Item)	By Whom? (Office/Person)	By When? (Time Frame)	Resources, Required— Personnel, Supplies, Equipment, Programming, etc.	Estimated Costs

GRANTS OFFICE INVENTORY

Chapter 9 *(continued)*

The Role of the Grants Office in the Administration of Private Funds

For Each Activity/Item Listed, Check Status:

Activity/Item	Reviewed, Appropriate Part of Grants Office	Reviewed, Appropriate Part of Other Office (List)	Reviewed, Not Applicable	Reviewed, Inappropriate Needs Action	Non-existent, Needs Action
4. Budget modifications • designation of person or office responsible for obtaining and recording approval to reallocate funds disseminated by funding source • guidelines for requesting changes in budget allocations such					

Complete this Section for Each Activity/Item Needing Action:

What Needs to Be Accomplished? (Activity/Item)	By Whom? (Office/Person)	By When? (Time Frame)	Resources, Required—Personnel, Supplies, Equipment, Programming, etc.	Estimated Costs

GRANTS OFFICE INVENTORY
Chapter 9 (continued)
The Role of the Grants Office in the Administration of Private Funds

For Each Activity/Item Listed, Check Status:

Activity/Item	Reviewed, Appropriate Part of Grants Office	Reviewed, Appropriate Part of Other Office (List)	Reviewed, Not Applicable	Reviewed, Inappropriate Needs Action	Non-existent, Needs Action
as the use of a "letter of notice" 5. Equipment and pur-chasing controls • computerized or man-ual numbering system for all equipment pur-chased through private grant funds • designation of person or office responsible for					

Complete this Section for Each Activity/Item Needing Action:

What Needs to Be Accomplished? (Activity/Item)	By Whom? (Office/ Person)	By When? (Time Frame)	Resources, Required— Personnel, Supplies, Equipment, Programming, etc.	Estimated Costs

GRANTS OFFICE INVENTORY

Chapter 9 *(continued)*

The Role of the Grants Office in the Administration of Private Funds

For Each Activity/Item Listed, Check Status:

Activity/Item	Reviewed, Appropriate Part of Grants Office	Reviewed, Appropriate Part of Other Office (List)	Reviewed, Not Applicable	Reviewed, Inappropriate Needs Action	Non-existent, Needs Action
maintaining this system 6. Cash requests • designated person or office and written policy and procedures for negotiating the type of reimbursement with the funding source 7. Personnel requirements and procedures • designated person or					

Complete this Section for Each Activity/Item Needing Action:

What Needs to Be Accomplished? (Activity/Item)	By Whom? (Office/Person)	By When? (Time Frame)	Resources, Required—Personnel, Supplies, Equipment, Programming, etc.	Estimated Costs

GRANTS OFFICE INVENTORY
Chapter 9 *(continued)*
The Role of the Grants Office in the Administration of Private Funds

For Each Activity/Item Listed, Check Status:

Activity/Item	Reviewed, Appropriate Part of Grants Office	Reviewed, Appropriate Part of Other Office (List)	Reviewed, Not Applicable	Reviewed, Inappropriate Needs Action	Non-existent, Needs Action
office to handle personnel issues, payroll records, etc. • availability of personnel procedures accepted by the American Institute of Certified Public Accountants • use of standard payroll records for the expenditure of funds and					

Complete this Section for Each Activity/Item Needing Action:

What Needs to Be Accomplished? (Activity/Item)	By Whom? (Office/Person)	By When? (Time Frame)	Resources, Required—Personnel, Supplies, Equipment, Programming, etc.	Estimated Costs

GRANTS OFFICE INVENTORY

Chapter 9 *(continued)*

The Role of the Grants Office in the Administration of Private Funds

For Each Activity/Item Listed, Check Status:

Activity/Item	Reviewed, Appropriate Part of Grants Office	Reviewed, Appropriate Part of Other Office (List)	Reviewed, Not Applicable	Reviewed, Inappropriate Needs Action	Non-existent, Needs Action
the documentation of in-kind services and matching funds • written policy and procedures outlining fair employment practices					

Complete this Section for Each Activity/Item Needing Action:

What Needs to Be Accomplished? (Activity/Item)	By Whom? (Office/Person)	By When? (Time Frame)	Resources, Required— Personnel, Supplies, Equipment, Programming, etc.	Estimated Costs

CHAPTER 10

The Role of the Grants Office in the Administration of Federal Funds

When an application is approved for funding, the grants-management officer will prepare a Notice of Grant Award. Most negotiations on budget amounts will be done with the program officer before the Notice of Grant Award is issued.

Negotiating Grant Awards

Arguing against reductions in your original proposed budget is futile. You must relate changes in the final budget to the reduction or elimination of methods/activities and the effect of these reductions in the attainment of proposed objectives. Your project planner (Chapter 7) will provide the necessary linkage between activities and budget categories and amounts. Therefore, attach a project planner to your proposal whenever attachments are allowed, or send one to the program officer when the negotiation process begins.

Since federal government applications request information on project directors (e.g., name, phone number), the funding source may contact the project director or principal investigator directly to negotiate the budget. Some project directors have the skills necessary to negotiate a budget, but mistakes are more likely if the grants office is not involved in the process. To ensure fiscal integrity, it is imperative that your grants system mandate the inclusion of the grants office in *all* budget negotiations. Since the federal cover sheet includes the name of the fiscal agent, agents are usually included in the award process. The fiscal agent may be the business office and not the grants office. Both need to be informed.

In many cases, the program officer who has been the main contact in the grants process to this point appoints a member of his or her fiscal team to complete the budget. The federal fiscal representative is not concerned with objectives, protocol, or degrees of change in measurement indicators. He or she simply wants all of the columns to add up so the process of distributing the funds can begin. You may be successful in transferring funds by category, but the total amount of the award will be changed only with the intervention of the program officer.

The federal fiscal agent can answer your questions on allowable expenses (e.g., rental/purchase of equipment). In one grant I was involved with, the federal fiscal agent acted as the fiscal officer for both grants and contracts. When confronted with a question on how best to handle an equipment lease/rental agreement, the officer suggested we change our grant to a contract to allow the rent to apply toward the purchase of equipment. By starting out as a contract, we would not have to make changes later.

The best time to talk with a federal funding official is before the final award amount is determined, categories of funding designated, and forms signed. In some cases, the amount that the federal official announces as the total is fixed and nonnegotiable. In these instances, your project planner should be adjusted to reflect a realistic scope of work based on the size of the award.

Once final award amount and categories of funding are agreed upon, the type of payment must be decided.

Cash Requests

Grant funds are distributed through one of two methods of payment: direct treasury checks or letters of credit. Payments are made on either a cash-in-advance-of-expenditures or reimbursement basis.

The cash-in-advance system is preferable to the reimbursement method. The former does not require an organization to expend its own funds for items or services that will be reimbursed at a later date or force it to borrow interest-laden cash to meet project expenses. Your project planner and grants time line will help you develop monthly cash forecasts and estimates of your expenditure rate. These will assist you in meeting the federal regulations for cash advances.

Whether you are going to be paid by the cash-in-advance or reimbursement system, your financial management system must meet or exceed the accountability standard outlined in the following Office of Management and Budget (OMB) circulars:

- A–102 for state and local governments

- A–110 for nonprofit organizations (including nonprofit colleges, universities, hospitals, etc.)

You need to monitor your cash needs carefully:

- Limit the amount requested to the minimum required to accomplish your objective(s).

- Do not build up extra cash.

- Move the cash through your books swiftly.

- Deposit federal funds in minority banks.

As a result of the Paperwork Reduction Act Notice and the advances brought about by computers, the grants payment process has been simplified, and the time involved in mailing forms and checks has been greatly reduced. The following information has been taken from the Public Health Service Grants Policy Statement, DHHS Publication No. (OASH) 82–50,000 (Rev.), January 1, 1987.

Letters of Credit

The letter of credit authorizes a grantee to submit payment vouchers through its financial institution to the Treasury for credit of funds to the grantee's account at its financial institution. The request and resulting credit amounts are transmitted electronically through the Treasury Fiscal Communications System (TFCS). Requests for funds are normally processed the following work day. The letter of credit indicates the dollar amount available to a grantee during a specified period. Recipient eligibility for electronic payments of letters of credit is set forth in Treasury financial manuals. For a financial institution to service letters-of-credit accounts, it must be able to tie into the TFCS.

Monthly Cash Request (Treasury Checks)

Grantees that are not eligible for advance of funds by letter of credit are financed on a monthly cash-request basis. Under this method of payment, grantee organizations may request grant funds monthly, based on expected disbursements during the succeeding month and the amount of federal funds already on hand. For timely receipt of cash, a grantee's request must reach the Federal Assistance Financing Branch at least two weeks before the date the cash is needed.

Reimbursement by Treasury Check

Reimbursement financing is used for a few specifically designated programs, such as construction, and for those grantees who have abused advanced-funding privileges. For example, it would be used where it is determined that the grantee's financial management system does not meet the standard in 45 CFR 74, Subpart H, or that the grantee has not maintained, or demonstrated the willingness and ability to maintain, procedures that will minimize the time between transfer of funds from the Treasury and their disbursement for grant-related purposes.

Under this method, payment is made to the grantee with a Treasury check upon receipt of a request approved by an awarding office for reimbursement from the grantee. A request for reimbursement may be submitted monthly or more often if authorized.

Secondary Recipient Advances

Advances made by the grantee to subgrantee and contractor organizations must conform substantially to the same standards of timing and amount that govern advances made by the federal government to the grantee under the above-mentioned payment methods.

Assignment of Payments

When the grant provides for payment only after incurrence of costs (reimbursement-payment method), the alternatives discussed below regarding assignment and other means of ensuring adequate working capital are appropriate.

With approval of the awarding office, grant payments due or about to become due (under the types of grants indicated above) may be assigned to financial institutions under the following conditions:

1. The award provides for reimbursements totaling $1,000 or more.
2. The payments are assigned to a bank, trust company, or other financial institution, including any federal lending agency.
3. The program's legislation does not prohibit assignment.
4. The assignment covers all amounts payable under the grant that have not already been paid and are not subject to further assignment. (This does not preclude assignment to one party acting as agent or trustee for two or more parties participating in the financing.)
5. In the event of any assignment, the assignee shall file a written notice of grant payments assignment along with a true copy of the instrument of assignment with the awarding office and the responsible payment office.

Requests to assign payment should be submitted to the designated grants-management officer for approval. Upon approval, the grants-management officer will provide necessary information on how the assignment may be accomplished.

Any interest charges resulting from loans obtained on the basis of the assignment cannot be charged to project funds.

In instances where lack of federal funds due would cause a hardship on the grantee, it is possible to accelerate the grant payments. The grantee should contact the grants-management officer of the awarding office to request expeditious handling of its reimbursement request or to obtain authorization to submit reimbursement requests more often than monthly.

Grantees might also consider arranging a short-term loan from a lending institution in an amount sufficient for the initial phase of the grant-supported activity. Using the grant award as collateral, a grantee could secure such a loan and pay it off upon receipt of the federal payment. Grantees would have to absorb interest payments, but this would be for a lesser amount over a shorter period of time than that incurred by assigning grant payments. The process of securing short-term loans could be repeated if necessary.

Personnel Requirements and Procedures

The acceptance of federal funds requires the signature of assurances relating to the federal nondiscrimination laws. Most grantees are in such a rush that they do not think about the personnel forms they signed, nor do they recall all the assurances they signed months ago when they submitted the proposal.

These federal nondiscrimination laws are listed here because of their applicability to grants. They are not meant to be inclusive of the rules governing this area.

1. The National Labor Relations Act of 1935. Prohibits discrimination in certain employment practices on the bases of race and sex. This includes private employers and subcontractors.
2. Federal Communications Act. Prohibits discrimination in employment on the bases of race, color, national origin, sex, and religion. This is relevant to all organizations and entities regulated by the Federal Communications Commission (broadcasters, common carriers, cable-television operators, and private firms).
3. Title II of the Civil Rights Act of 1964. Prohibits discrimination in the use of public accommodations on the bases of race, color, religion, and national origin. This is pertinent to all private organizations providing public accommodations.
4. Title VI of the Civil Rights Act of 1964. Provides that no person in the United States shall, on the base of race, color, or national origin, be excluded from the participation in, be denied benefits of, or be subjected to discrimination under any programs or activity receiving federal financial assistance.
5. Title IX of the Civil Rights Act of 1870, Civil Rights Act of 1964. Prohibits use of state custom or law to deprive individuals and organizations in the United States of civil rights for any reason.
6. Civil Rights Act of 1866. Prohibits discrimination in real estate transactions on the bases of race and color. Refers to all organizations and individuals engaged in real estate transactions.
7. Apprenticeship Amendments of 1973. Prohibits discrimination in employment of the bases of race, color, religion, sex, and

national origin. Refers to apprenticeship programs registered
with the Department of Labor.

8. Age Discrimination in Employment Act of 1975. Prohibits discrimination in employment on the basis of age. Refers to private
employers, state and local government, and labor organizations.

9. Section 504 of Rehabilitation Act of 1973. Provides that no
otherwise qualified handicapped individual in the United States
shall solely by reason of the handicap be excluded from any
program receiving federal financial assistance.

10. Title IX of Education Amendments of 1972 (Section 901). Prohibits age discrimination in education programs receiving federal
financial assistance.

Common Personnel Problems Related to Grants

Most smaller organizations use their personnel department to
handle grant-related employees as well as those on their regular
payroll. There are issues with grant-related staff that are different
from those of regular staff, and the personnel department needs to
be aware of them.

1. Compliance with grantor regulations. Read over the guidelines
and circulars that relate to personnel policy and decisions and
forward them to the personnel director.

2. Grant-funded employees must face the fact that the grant *will
eventually end*. Their performance on the grant may have little
relationship to the continuation of the grant. Even if they work
particularly hard, efficiently, and loyally, the grant will end, and
they will have to face locating another job.

3. The grants area has always been weak in the employee-evaluation
area. Performance measures and evaluations are rarely outlined
in advance. However, assurance is given that grant-related employees will be treated the same as the regular staff, and therefore,
if the regular employees undergo evaluation, so must the grant
employees.

4. High job turnover is common in the grants area. It is natural
for individuals to want job security, and the anxiety of grant
renewals and so on takes its toll.

Many of the techniques in Chapter 4 on the motivation of staff
will produce great benefits with grant staff. Review that section and

you may find ways to overcome some of the problems that arise when grant employees are not treated the same as nongrant-funded staff. Your efforts in developing a good work atmosphere will avoid grievances and law suits.

In an effort to attract employees to work on a grant, you may offer different pay scales. Some grant jobs pay more to encourage *loyalty* to complete the grant (high risk, high pay). This practice can irritate the regular employees and the union and cause motivation problems. Just remember, the most important rules to obey are those of the grantor.

Procurement and Control

The basic requirements for procurement are outlined in OMB circulars A–110 and A–102. In addition to the appropriate OMB circulars governing the area of employment, review the Public Health Service Grants Policy Statement, DHHS Publication No. OASH 82–50,000 1/1/87, and the Federal Acquisition Regulation (FAR) for a deeper understanding of the area.

GRANTS OFFICE INVENTORY

Chapter 10

The Role of the Grants Office in the Administration of Federal Funds

For Each Activity/Item Listed, Check Status:

Activity/Item	Reviewed, Appropriate Part of Grants Office	Reviewed, Appropriate Part of Other Office (List)	Reviewed, Not Applicable	Reviewed, Inappropriate Needs Action	Non-existent, Needs Action
1. Negotiating grant awards • designation of person or office to handle all budget negotiations • policy to relate all changes in the budget to the reduction or elimination of methods/activities and the					

Complete this Section for Each Activity/Item Needing Action:

What Needs to Be Accomplished? (Activity/Item)	By Whom? (Office/Person)	By When? (Time Frame)	Resources, Required— Personnel, Supplies, Equipment, Programming, etc.	Estimated Costs

GRANTS OFFICE INVENTORY

Chapter 10 (continued)

The Role of the Grants Office in the Administration of Federal Funds

For Each Activity/Item Listed, Check Status:

Activity/Item	Reviewed, Appropriate Part of Grants Office	Reviewed, Appropriate Part of Other Office (List)	Reviewed, Not Applicable	Reviewed, Inappropriate Needs Action	Non-existent, Needs Action
attainment of objectives (use of project planner) 2. Cash requests • designation of person or office to handle all cash requests • existence of financial management system that meets or exceeds the accountability standards outlined in					

Complete this Section for Each Activity/Item Needing Action:

What Needs to Be Accomplished? (Activity/Item)	By Whom? (Office/Person)	By When? (Time Frame)	Resources, Required— Personnel, Supplies, Equipment, Programming, etc.	Estimated Costs

195

GRANTS OFFICE INVENTORY
Chapter 10 *(continued)*
The Role of the Grants Office in the Administration of Federal Funds

For Each Activity/Item Listed, Check Status:

Activity/Item	Reviewed, Appropriate Part of Grants Office	Reviewed, Appropriate Part of Other Office (List)	Reviewed, Not Applicable	Reviewed, Inappropriate Needs Action	Non-existent, Needs Action
the appropriate OMB circulars 3. Personnel requirements and procedures • designation of person or office to handle grant related employees and ensure compliance to federal nondiscrimination laws					

Complete this Section for Each Activity/Item Needing Action:

What Needs to Be Accomplished? (Activity/Item)	By Whom? (Office/Person)	By When? (Time Frame)	Resources, Required—Personnel, Supplies, Equipment, Programming, etc.	Estimated Costs

GRANTS OFFICE INVENTORY

Chapter 10 (continued)

The Role of the Grants Office in the Administration of Federal Funds

For Each Activity/Item Listed, Check Status:

Activity/Item	Reviewed, Appropriate Part of Grants Office	Reviewed, Appropriate Part of Other Office (List)	Reviewed, Not Applicable	Reviewed, Inappropriate Needs Action	Non-existent, Needs Action
4. Procurement and control • designated person or office to ensure that the basic requirements for procurement are adhered to • availability of appropriate: OMB circulars, Public Health Service grants					

Complete this Section for Each Activity/Item Needing Action:

What Needs to Be Accomplished? (Activity/Item)	By Whom? (Office/ Person)	By When? (Time Frame)	Resources, Required— Personnel, Supplies, Equipment, Programming, etc.	Estimated Costs

GRANTS OFFICE INVENTORY

Chapter 10 *(continued)*

The Role of the Grants Office in the Administration of Federal Funds

For Each Activity/Item Listed, Check Status:

Activity/Item	Reviewed, Appropriate Part of Grants Office	Reviewed, Appropriate Part of Other Office (List)	Reviewed, Not Applicable	Reviewed, Inappropriate Needs Action	Non-existent, Needs Action
Policy Statements, and Federal Acquisition Regulations					

Complete this Section for Each Activity/Item Needing Action:

What Needs to Be Accomplished? (Activity/Item)	By Whom? (Office/Person)	By When? (Time Frame)	Resources, Required— Personnel, Supplies, Equipment, Programming, etc.	Estimated Costs

CHAPTER 11

Indirect Cost Recovery

by
MARY L. OTTO

Projects funded by external agencies are divided into direct- and indirect-cost categories. Throughout this chapter reference is made to college and university research efforts and the recovery of indirect costs. However, other nonprofit organizations conducting grants and contracts are also eligible to uncover these costs. In some colleges and universities, the indirect-cost calculations and negotiations are the responsibility of the research office, and in others they are done by the business office. The research administration office must be familiar with the process for determining indirect costs and must understand its purpose. Research administrators are often called upon to provide information on direct and indirect costs to faculty, other administrators, and representatives from the community.

Direct costs are those that are specifically related to the project. For example, direct costs on a funded project include salaries, supplies, travel, and equipment. The direct costs are itemized in the proposal budget with a justification for each line item.

Indirect costs include expenses that are less obviously related to the project but are none-the-less necessary to support the environment in which the project takes place. Such costs include plant operations, the business and accounting office, purchasing, the personnel office, research administration, and departmental administration. Indirect costs are charged to externally funded projects to recover incremental costs incurred by the institution to support the research project. In order to receive indirect-cost reimbursement, an institution must have an approved permanent rate. Although indirect costs will be awarded by funding agencies to institutions with provisional or past permanent rates, the payment will be disallowed if the institution fails to establish an effective permanent rate.

The support services of the institution are not specific to each project. Therefore, the cost must be averaged and applied evenly to all the projects supported by the university. These services help to create the institution's capacity for research and academic projects. The indirect costs charged to each project, then, are reimbursements for the expenses the university incurs to provide a research environment.

There are several publications produced by the Office of Management and Budget (OMB) that give information on indirect-cost and budget regulations. Among the most frequently used are OMB circular A–110 and A–21. The Public Health Service (PHS) transmittal 87.02, issued August 25, 1987, provides information on indirect-cost reimbursement for all PHS grants awarded after October 1, 1987. The National Association of College and University Business Officers (NACUBO) offers publications that explain the preparation of indirect-cost studies and rate proposals. In conjunction with several professional associations, NACUBO offers workshops on postaward administration and indirect-cost studies. A research administrator, whether or not directly involved in the post-award administration and indirect-cost calculation, should attend one of these workshops every three to five years to remain knowledgeable about the guidelines for indirect costs.

The indirect-cost calculation begins with the categorization of expenditures of indirect cost into homogenous cost pools. Indirect-cost pools include the use allowances of buildings and equipment, operations and maintenance of plant, sponsored project administration, library, and other units. OMB regulations require that a base be established for each of the cost pools. The base cost is then apportioned to reasonably represent its benefit to major institutional activities such as research and instruction. These costs are converted into a rate that is applied to each grant and contract awarded to the institution.

The final indirect-cost rate is negotiated between the Department of Health and Human Services (DHHS) or the Office of Naval Research (ONR) and the institution. Once agreement is reached, the institution receives an indirect-cost rate agreement stating the negotiated indirect cost for its research and instruction. The indirect-cost reimbursement agreement is issued for a specified period of time, usually no less than one year and no more than three. When the institution is satisfied with the rate, it is sometimes better to negotiate the longest possible time period to avoid the time-consuming task of completing additional indirect-cost studies.

The indirect-cost study must be submitted promptly to avoid penalties from funding agencies. If a funding agency declares that an institution is unreasonably delinquent in submitting its indirect-cost proposal for review, the agency may elect not to reimburse indirect costs during the period of delinquency.

Sometimes the physical and/or administrative environment in which certain activities are performed require the establishment of an off-campus rate for the institution. The on-campus rate applies to projects conducted on the campus; the off-campus rate applies to projects at an off-campus site. The off-campus rate can be established for a specific location, or it can be one rate that applies to all off-campus sites. When an off-campus location is identified with a specific rate, the rate applies only to those activities conducted at that site. The indirect-cost rate agreement specifies the circumstances under which activities are eligible for an off-campus rate.

A project that takes place both off and on campus is usually designated as an on-campus or off-campus project according to where the majority of the work will be done. Alternatively, an institution may charge on-campus rates to each component of the project completed on campus and off-campus rates to each component completed off campus. The indirect-cost rate agreement normally specifies the treatment of partially off-campus projects. If it does not, the treatment accorded the project by the grantee is generally accepted subject to an audit.

The reimbursement of indirect costs on training grants is limited to 8 percent of the total direct cost unless the institution agrees to a lower rate. *Training grants* are any grants that provide support for educational services and training, such as summer institutes, the development and introduction of new courses, community workshops, and research training programs. The 8 percent training rate applies to any proposed training program that requests federal support.

Indirect costs generally are not reimbursed on awards for equipment, construction, and conferences. Fellowship or tuition awards to faculty or students are usually made for a fixed amount or to cover the actual cost and do not reimburse indirect costs.

Funding agencies set an award amount for each project, including direct- and indirect-cost figures. This total dollar figure then constitutes the ceiling on the amount available for the project. The investigator and the institution may request increased funds, but the agency is not obligated to make supplemental awards. After an award is made, most agencies will adjust the indirect-cost allocation to an institution as soon as its indirect-cost rate is established. Adjustments are likely if the institution is in the process of indirect negotiating its cost rate when the project proposal is submitted to the agency. Funds to cover indirect costs associated with an additional direct-cost award for expansion, extension, or other reasons may be given at the discretion of the agency.

Institutions may transfer funds meant for direct costs to indirect costs and vice versa without prior approval from a federal funding agency as long as the objectives of the project remain the same. If an investigator or the institution desires to change the objectives or scope of the project, approval is required. Agency approval is also required under other prior-approval requirements, such as the purchase of equipment costing more than $25,000.

If an institution has never established an indirect-cost rate, it must submit an indirect-cost proposal to the regional Division of Cost Allocation (DCA). Specific directions for the proposal preparation are available from the regional DCA and the other sources referred to earlier. The rate negotiator works with the institutional representative to negotiate a reimbursement rate. The proposal for an indirect-cost reimbursement rate should be submitted and approved prior to the submission of grant proposals to federal agencies. However, it is possible to submit the indirect cost and grant proposals at the same time or even to submit the indirect proposal after the grant proposal. If an indirect-cost rate is not established prior to the grant award, a provisional award will be included for one-half the requested rate up to the maximum allowable percentage of direct salaries and wages supported by the agency. The funding agency reserves the balance of the requested indirect-cost rate. If a rate is established, the additional funds for the difference will be awarded based on the approval rate.

Faculty tend to have a negative attitude toward indirect cost. They often operate under the misconception that the indirect-cost portion of their grant constitutes a profit to the institution. In truth, universities never recover all of the costs related to research.

Since indirect costs cannot be identified with the investigator's project, the value of the institution's operations to a particular project is frequently questioned. In some cases, the investigator may claim that a project uses *some* of the institution's resources but not as many resources as other researchers. It is important to be able to explain that indirect cost is an average of all the costs of providing support to the various projects. Some projects will use more resources, and others will use less.

Some faculty believe that the indirect-cost rate interferes with their competitive position in seeking external funds. Although federal agencies handle indirect-cost recovery in a variety of ways, all agencies are familiar with indirect-cost recovery requirements. Thus faculty are not disadvantaged by the institution's indirect-cost rate. Businesses/industries, hospitals, state agencies, and private foundations have different rules governing the allocation of indirect-cost recovery. For example, some foundations refuse to refund any indirect costs and some business and industries refund 100 percent of the indirect costs related to research projects funded by them. The research administration office at each institution must be familiar with sponsor guidelines on indirect cost.

SUMMARY

Research administrators should be familiar with the purpose of indirect-cost allocations and how they are used to support university research and academic projects. The indirect costs charged to externally funded projects reimburse some of the university's additional costs to provide support services for externally funded projects. The following Indirect Cost Information Sheet will help you determine what cost areas need attention at your institution, and how to answer faculty and staff questions concerning indirect costs.

INDIRECT-COST INFORMATION SHEET

Q. Why are indirect costs charged to my project?

A. Indirect costs provide reimbursement to the university for support required for your project and others like it.

Q. Since payroll and other services have to be available whether or not my project is funded, why does my project have to pay for them?

A. These services create an environment that makes it possible for your project to exist on the campus. Although your project alone does not create a need for increased services, extra services are required to support all the externally funded projects.

Q. My research project is quite simple, requiring only office space and the use of the library. Why is the indirect cost the same as for laboratory research projects?

A. The indirect-cost rate is an average of all the costs of providing support to various projects. Some projects use more resources, and others use less.

Q. Doesn't the university actually make money on the indirect-cost reimbursement?

A. No. The university actually recovers only a portion of the actual cost to support all the combined externally funded projects.

Q. Why doesn't the university recover all its costs for supporting externally funded projects?

A. Universities do not expect to recover all of the costs associated with externally funded projects because they have a commitment to providing a scholarly environment that supports research.

GRANTS OFFICE INVENTORY
Chapter 11
Indirect Cost Recovery

For Each Activity/Item Listed, Check Status:

Activity/Item	Reviewed, Appropriate Part of Grants Office	Reviewed, Appropriate Part of Other Office (List)	Reviewed, Not Applicable	Reviewed, Inappropriate Needs Action	Non-existent, Needs Action
1. Institution has approved indirect cost rate. 2. Copy of the indirect cost rate agreement is made available to project directors, research administrators, grant writers, etc. 3. Designated person or office to ensure that					

Complete this Section for Each Activity/Item Needing Action:

What Needs to Be Accomplished? (Activity/Item)	By Whom? (Office/ Person)	By When? (Time Frame)	Resources, Required— Personnel, Supplies, Equipment, Programming, etc.	Estimated Costs

GRANTS OFFICE INVENTORY

Chapter 11 *(continued)*
Indirect Cost Recovery

For Each Activity/Item Listed, Check Status:

Activity/Item	Reviewed, Appropriate Part of Grants Office	Reviewed, Appropriate Part of Other Office (List)	Reviewed, Not Applicable	Reviewed, Inappropriate Needs Action	Non-existent, Needs Action
the indirect cost rate is utilized in all applicable proposals 4. Designated person or office to negotiate the indirect cost rate 5. Policy and procedures outlining who has a say in what is included in the institution's cost pools					

Complete this Section for Each Activity/Item Needing Action:

What Needs to Be Accomplished? (Activity/Item)	By Whom? (Office/ Person)	By When? (Time Frame)	Resources, Required— Personnel, Supplies, Equipment, Programming, etc.	Estimated Costs

GRANTS OFFICE INVENTORY

Chapter 11 *(continued)*
Indirect Cost Recovery

For Each Activity/Item Listed, Check Status:

Activity/Item	Reviewed, Appropriate Part of Grants Office	Reviewed, Appropriate Part of Other Office (List)	Reviewed, Not Applicable	Reviewed, Inappropriate Needs Action	Non-existent, Needs Action
6. Designated person or office to offer explanations to faculty/staff about the purpose of indirect cost reimbursement (provision of fact sheet, etc.)					

Complete this Section for Each Activity/Item Needing Action:

What Needs to Be Accomplished? (Activity/Item)	By Whom? (Office/ Person)	By When? (Time Frame)	Resources, Required— Personnel, Supplies, Equipment, Programming, etc.	Estimated Costs

CHAPTER 12

The Role of the Grants Office in the Politics of the Funding Process

Public Funds—Keeping the Door Open

Many grants offices perform a variety of valuable functions that center on protecting the funding opportunities currently available to their organizations. While lobbyists and national associations are usually concerned with creating new opportunities, the grants office may be actively involved or contribute to these activities in a support role.

According to our legislative process, bills are introduced and voted upon, and some become law. Legislation at both the state and federal level is introduced through your state or federal elected officials, concerned groups, associations, or lobbyists.

To have an impact on the system, you must be able to have an impact on the key individuals who will influence the legislation quickly and effectively. Smaller nonprofit organizations rely extensively on association or membership groups to provide this legislative function. However, problems can occur if the legislative staff person for the association is not a grants person. In this case, the process of appropriation of funds and the rules that govern who is the legal recipient of the funds may not allow your organization to compete.

208

After laws are passed, the state or federal bill must go through a committee process that designates which program will be appropriated funds under an agency's budget. Tracking the progress of your program through this process is complex and tedious. Many reports, hearings, and compromises occur along the way.

What may seem a trivial change may result in disastrous effects on your favorite grant program. Consider what happened recently in a program for colleges and universities. Through this program, millions of dollars were appropriated annually to fund both two-year and four-year institutions. Originally, two-year colleges were designated to receive a percentage of the funds so that the larger four-year institutions did not take it all. However, a change was initiated, and a dollar figure was substituted for the percentage. At first glance the dollar figure looked commensurate with past years' percentages. But the appropriation to the program ended up being significantly less than it had been in previous years. Since the dollar figure, and not the percentage, for two-year colleges was in the bill, two-year colleges received the dollar amount, which left the four-year colleges with almost nothing.

Understanding the system, and how bills and appropriations result in grants that your organization is eligible to apply for, is critically important to the "health" of your grants system.

SUBVERSION OF THE GRANTS SYSTEM

Unfortunately, it has become increasingly common to subvert the grants system through the political process. While publicity concerning this subversion has been relatively recent, this abuse has been around for a long time. At the risk of further publicizing the abuse and hence increasing it, I have chosen to include this section with the hope that the astute grants administrator will see that such abuse puts our grants system in jeopardy.

I first became aware of the subversion of the grants-award process in the early 1970s. A proposal of mine was next to be funded when the federal funding agency ran out of money. My boss instructed me to pursue funding. The federal agency told me to apply again next year. Then I read that the same federal agency had just awarded another nonprofit group a grant for $1 million! I flew to Washington, D.C., went directly to the agency director, and was told that the funded organization had not been on the list of prospective grantees and had not undergone peer review. What the organization did do was convince their federal representative to add a provision to a popular bill that earmarked, or designated, $1 million to be awarded to their organization to fund their project. This process of legislating grants not only sidesteps the grants-review process but also has the potential of dismantling peer review and the entire grant award system.

While the entrepreneurial grant seeker who espouses survival of the fittest may say that all is fair in developing resources for your organization, the practice of adding grants to every congressperson's and senator's bills causes chaos. Fortunately, many executives of nonprofit organizations have refused to accept grants acquired through a noncompetitive system.

This chapter encourages the director of the grants effort to determine who in the organization will facilitate the appropriation of grant funds. A knowledge of the federal funding mechanism will assist your organization in assigning the task of influencing the grants mechanism.

GRANT-RELATED RULES

The Federal Register prints announcements stating opportunities to comment on the rules that govern what types of organizations are eligible to apply for and receive federal funds, the review system, priorities, and so on. Newly created funding programs must offer opportunities to participate in the development of the rules. Existing programs must announce opportunities to comment on last year's rules, rule changes, and the issuing of final rules.

Action: Alert appropriate administrators, associations, and agencies of the necessity to submit favorable and unfavorable comments on the rules. Since few people actively track the grants system at this level, federal officials receive very few comments. When they receive a few, they assume that there are many more individuals who feel the same but did not respond. Remember, rules that affect you dramatically may be changed based on the comments of a few.

FEDERAL REVENUE SHARING AND FORMULA GRANTS DESIGNED TO DISTRIBUTE FUNDS TO INDIVIDUAL STATES

States are required to sponsor hearings on the expenditure of federal funds that pass through the state to nonprofit organizations.

Action: Review your organization's current grants to determine what monies are now derived under this federal funding mechanism and designate an individual to testify at appropriate hearings.

PUBLIC HEARINGS (STATE AND FEDERAL)

The Federal Register announces public hearings on federal funding programs. Testifying at and/or attending these hearings may result in several advantages for your organization, including appropriations. Many state priorities are developed from testimony and comments made at state hearings.

Action: The grants office may schedule a trip to your state capital or to Washington, D.C. Alert the appropriate staff to the hearing dates and ask them to attend.

CONTACTING ELECTED OFFICIALS

In this activity, the grants office monitors all contact with funding sources to exert influence and increase elected officials' knowledge of:

- the organization's "official" position on a particular area
- the need for funding (letters sent from administrators, board directors, etc.)

Action: This may entail more than monitoring contact. The grants administrator may track legislation and appropriations and *initiate* the appropriate response. This may include drafting letters from your organization's officials to sending telegrams and even visiting federal and state officials.

Webbing and Linkages to Elected Officials

The advantage of a system of developing and recording linkages to federal funding sources has been discussed in Chapter 5. Extrapolate that system to include state and federal elected officials in an attempt to introduce grant-related legislation favorable to your organization.

It is recommended that your linkages system with elected officials be carried out separately from your linkages system with grant officials.

Review with your board, advisory committees, volunteers, and staff the importance of discussing with elected officials the concerns and needs of your organization so that they may be addressed in bills and appropriations. After review of the purpose of the activity and reassurance that *you will not contact any of their linkages* without *their* permission, you are ready to distribute the Elected Officials Linkage Worksheet at the end of this section.

You may decide to leave the elected officials section of the worksheet blank for the respondent to complete, or you may list the names of those officials you are particularly interested in.

Record the information collected from the worksheets in a special data-retrieval system that can be secured to restrict access of usage. When the occasion to act on a legislative issue arises, the information contained in your system will help you design your political strategy quickly. Who do you know who can reach the official? Linkages, including names, addresses, and phone numbers, are easily retrieved for your action plans.

Politics of Corporations

In addition to setting up a webbing and linkage system with political officials and funding officials of foundations, corporations, and government programs, you must take into consideration local corporate politics. Your webbing system, discussed in Chapter 5, will yield contact people to assist in approaching corporations, but it's also important to be aware of the politics of corporate commitment to your community and your organization.

You can gain this knowledge by:

- buying shares of corporate stock

- tracking corporate officials

- logging financial reports, Dunn and Bradstreet reports, etc.

- cataloging annual reports

- contracting with a clipping service to collect news articles on the corporation

In some cases, the development office may record this information. However, in most nonprofits the information is scattered throughout the organization in a variety of offices. It is useful for the grants office to know:

- what banks handle your organization's checking and savings accounts

- what companies handle your endowments/investments

- who your organization's major suppliers are for materials, equipment, etc.

Remember that your business office and purchasing departments are probably asking your major suppliers for their best price, thereby lowering their profits. Therefore, you must show a little discretion when requesting contributions from them. However, this does not mean you should not ask. After all, they always have the option of declining your request.

ELECTED OFFICIALS LINKAGE WORKSHEET

Your Name _____

Your Address _____

Your Phone Number _____

1. What political party do you belong to?

   _____

2. Have you worked on an elected official's campaign?   Yes   No

   If yes, whose? _____

   _____

3. Did you make campaign contributions to any of the candidates currently in office?
   Yes   No

   If yes, please put $ next to name(s) on list

4. Do you know any of the current office holders?   Yes   No

   If yes, put an * next to name(s) on list

5. Do you know anyone that knows any of the current officeholders?   Yes   No

   If yes, please list.

Name	Official
_____	_____
_____	_____
_____	_____

6. Please list any other information you may know about an elected official(s), such as educational background, military background, religious affiliations, etc.

   _____

   _____

STATE LEGISLATORS

_____

_____

_____

_____

FEDERAL CONGRESSPERSONS

_____

_____

_____

(SENATORS:)

_____

_____

STAFF (ADMIN. ASST.)

_____

_____

_____

COUNTY OFFICIALS

_____

_____

_____

CITY OFFICIALS

_____

_____

GRANTS OFFICE INVENTORY
Chapter 12
The Role of the Grants Office in the Politics of the Funding Process

For Each Activity/Item Listed, Check Status:

Activity/Item	Reviewed, Appropriate Part of Grants Office	Reviewed, Appropriate Part of Other Office (List)	Reviewed, Not Applicable	Reviewed, Inappropriate Needs Action	Non-existent, Needs Action
1. Availability of written materials explaining how bills and appropriations result in grants that your organization is eligible to apply for 2. Designation of individual or office to: • track legislation • facilitate the appropriation of grant funds					

Complete this Section for Each Activity/Item Needing Action:

What Needs to Be Accomplished? (Activity/Item)	By Whom? (Office/ Person)	By When? (Time Frame)	Resources, Required— Personnel, Supplies, Equipment, Programming, etc.	Estimated Costs

GRANTS OFFICE INVENTORY

Chapter 12 *(continued)*

The Role of the Grants Office in the Politics of the Funding Process

For Each Activity/Item Listed, Check Status:

Activity/Item	Reviewed, Appropriate Part of Grants Office	Reviewed, Appropriate Part of Other Office (List)	Reviewed, Not Applicable	Reviewed, Inappropriate Needs Action	Non-existent, Needs Action
• monitor possible attempts to subvert the grants system through the political process • monitor announcements concerning opportunities to comment on grant related rules • alert appropriate individuals, groups, etc.					

Complete this Section for Each Activity/Item Needing Action:

What Needs to Be Accomplished? (Activity/Item)	By Whom? (Office/Person)	By When? (Time Frame)	Resources, Required—Personnel, Supplies, Equipment, Programming, etc.	Estimated Costs

GRANTS OFFICE INVENTORY
Chapter 12 *(continued)*
The Role of the Grants Office in the Politics of the Funding Process

For Each Activity/Item Listed, Check Status:

Activity/Item	Reviewed, Appropriate Part of Grants Office	Reviewed, Appropriate Part of Other Office (List)	Reviewed, Not Applicable	Reviewed, Inappropriate Needs Action	Non-existent, Needs Action
of the necessity to submit comments on grant related rules • attend and testify at hearings on federal funding programs • monitor all contact with elected officials 3. System to record and monitor linkages to					

Complete this Section for Each Activity/Item Needing Action:

What Needs to Be Accomplished? (Activity/Item)	By Whom? (Office/ Person)	By When? (Time Frame)	Resources, Required— Personnel, Supplies, Equipment, Programming, etc.	Estimated Costs

GRANTS OFFICE INVENTORY
Chapter 12 *(continued)*
The Role of the Grants Office in the Politics of the Funding Process

For Each Activity/Item Listed, Check Status:

Activity/Item	Reviewed, Appropriate Part of Grants Office	Reviewed, Appropriate Part of Other Office (List)	Reviewed, Not Applicable	Reviewed, Inappropriate Needs Action	Non-existent, Needs Action
state and federal elected officials. • availability of data retrieval system that restricts access of usage 4. Designated individual or office to coordinate, record and monitor corporate research					

Complete this Section for Each Activity/Item Needing Action:

What Needs to Be Accomplished? (Activity/Item)	By Whom? (Office/Person)	By When? (Time Frame)	Resources, Required— Personnel, Supplies, Equipment, Programming, etc.	Estimated Costs

CHAPTER 13

The Grants Administrator

The grants administrator plays a different role in each organization. While there are many similarities, the differences and added functions are a result of the past and present administrations and how they perceive and have perceived the relative importance of the functions outlined in the preceding twelve chapters. A new president, chief executive officer, or director may call for a reordering of the functions of the grants office to fit his or her idea of what the office's priorities should be and what the grants administrator's job description should include.

The objective of this book is not to impart the idea that there is a perfect structure for grants administration or the grants office. The structure of the grants office, and where and how it fits into your administrative system, is based upon the functions that those individuals responsible for the administration decide the office should have. The grants administrator or other responsible official may decide that the inventory suggested at the end of each chapter should be periodically reviewed to insure the health of the grants effort in the same way an individual undergoes a yearly physical examination.

You will strengthen your grants system by performing the analysis suggested by each chapter's inventory. Individuals outside of the grants office may be assigned tasks that are revealed through the analysis. The inventory sheets suggest the resources that need to be provided along with the responsibilities and tasks that should be included in the job descriptions of these outside people.

The role of the grants administrator will be determined by compiling the grants office inventories at the end of each chapter. Place each of the duties or tasks that are to be the responsibility of the grants administrator on a Project Planner (see Chapter 7). The sample provided at the conclusion of this chapter was developed from the analysis of a grants position that did not require an emphasis on the accounting functions sometimes found in a grants office. The job was designed to promote and expand the number of proposals developed and the amount of funds granted.

The project planner should include the resources listed on the bottom of each inventory sheet. A job description should then be composed from the list of identified tasks. Due to the diversity of these tasks, recruiting an individual who has both the requisite educational background and personality characteristics can be problematic. A grants administrator with an accounting background, knowledge of federal grant rules, experience in budget preparation, skills in sales and marketing techniques, and appreciation for pre-proposal contact with funders may be difficult to find.

In the sample, the analysis of the project planner resulted in the job description entitled Director of Extramural Funding and Grants Management. A yearly performance evaluation uncovered the need to add the task of initiating a webbing and linkage system as discussed in Chapter 6. The project planner was changed, resources added, the job description adjusted, and a new year embarked upon.

The structure of the grants office should follow the functions that are determined to be the office's priorities. The functions must make allowance for the consideration of human factors such as finding a person who enjoys accomplishing these functions.

Individuals need to know the level of performance that is required for maintaining their positions. Most job advertisements do not state performance indicators, because most job descriptions do not. A review of the following job descriptions entitled "Proposal- and Resource-Development Specialist" and "Director of Contract and Grant Development" reveals differences in expectations although there are no stated measurement indicators for satisfactory levels of accomplishment. These job descriptions need to be accompanied by a project planner and an outline of the resources the successful candidate will command to reach the desired levels of performance.

Employing the techniques and strategies that culminate in this chapter will provide a grants system that serves your organization in a meaningful and measurable way. Your staff will develop realistic expectations of the grants office, and those employed in the grants system will understand what is expected of them. Morale will improve. Burn out and mistakes will be reduced and order will triumph over chaos. However, remember that just as this state is approached, a change will probably occur and an adjustment will have to be made. The system is not perfect, and the ever changing nature of our work will constantly create new demands.

The strategies outlined in this book have come from several years of consulting in grants administration. Over the past two decades, I have assisted many organizations and institutions in developing improved grant systems, thereby furthering causes and promoting better work atmospheres. I hope that these benefits also accrue to you and your organization as you begin to review and implement these strategies.

PROJECT PLANNER ™

BAUER ASSOCIATES

PROJECT TITLE: GRANTS COORDINATION   PROJECT DIRECTOR: RESEARCH COORDINATOR   DATE: 10/88 to 12/89

A — OBJECTIVES (What are you going to accomplish?)	B — ACTIVITIES • ACTION STEPS • METHODS (How will you do it?)	DATE C/D BEGIN/END	E WEEKS	F — WHO (will do it?)	PERSONNEL COSTS — G SALARIES & WAGES	FRINGE BENEFITS (H % OR $)	I TOTAL	CONSULTANTS • CONTRACT SERVICES — J WEEKS	K COST/WEEK	L TOTAL	NON-PERSONNEL RESOURCES NEEDED (SUPPLIES • EQUIPMENT • MATERIALS) — M ITEM	N COST/ITEM	O QUANTITY	P TOT COST	Q SUB-TOTAL COST FOR ACTIVITY / TOTAL I.L.P	MILESTONES PROGRESS INDICATORS — R ITEM	S DATE
A. Develop Staff Interest in Grants	A-1 Assist staff in developing a profile of their grants interests for research, demonstration projects, equipment needs, etc.	1/3		Research Coordinator and Project Secretary													
	a) Search for possible funding sources. a-1 Set up office to utilize Dialog Searching Service										modem and search budget for Dialog			3,000			
	a-2 Attend training seminar for Dialog										Travel for Dialog Training			500			
	b) Review staff research interests and produce an area profile by specialty.																
	c) Meet with divisions to determine how grants can assist in meeting division goals.																
	d) Meet with individual researchers to brainstorm projects																
	e) Suggest areas of emphasis or combined areas to increase grants potential.																
	A-2 Produce a "Department Research Review" to be disseminated monthly at faculty/staff meetings	3/12		Research Coordinator and Project Secretary							Printing / Reproduction Expense			1,000			

LIST KEY PERSONNEL POSITION	WEEKS ON PROJECT	SALARY/WEEK	NO. OF CLIENTS SERVED		COSTS REQUESTED FROM FUNDER ▲		% OF TOTAL
			COST PER CLIENT	U	DONATED COSTS ▲		▼ ▼ ▼
					TOTAL COSTS ▲		100%

INDIRECT COSTS AVAILABLE UNDER THE GRANT ARE: _____ % TDC x BOX T _____ = _____ OR _____ % S & W x BOX U _____ =

222

PROJECT PLANNER™

BAUER ASSOCIATES

PROJECT TITLE: GRANTS COORDINATION

PROJECT DIRECTOR: RESEARCH COORDINATOR

DATE: 12/88 rc 12/89

OBJECTIVES (What are you going to accomplish?) A	ACTIVITIES • ACTION STEPS • METHODS (How will you do it?) B	DATE BEGIN / END C/D	WEEKS E	WHO (will do it?) F
	a) Gather data for grants newsletter (Department Research Review).			
	b) Coordinate Newsletter:			
	b-1 To promote an increased awareness of the role that sponsored programs play in the Department			
	b-2 To promote an increased appreciation for the grant seekers who produce proposals			
	A-3 Develop pre-proposal review procedure with Research Committee and develop ongoing review system.	1/2		Research Coordinator and staff members (Research Committee.)
	a) Review procedures of existing Research Committee. Examine ways to assist and improve process.			
	A-4 Develop research goals with staff and Research Committee.	1/3		Research Coordinator and staff members
	a) Review the goals of the department list			

PERSONNEL COSTS

SALARIES & WAGES G	FRINGE BENEFITS % OR $ H	TOTAL I

CONSULTANTS • CONTRACT SERVICES

WEEKS J	COST/WEEK K	TOTAL L

NON-PERSONNEL RESOURCES NEEDED
SUPPLIES • EQUIPMENT • MATERIALS

ITEM M	COST/ITEM N	QUANTITY O	TOT COST P

SUB-TOTAL COST FOR ACTIVITY TOTAL I.L.P Q

MILESTONES / PROGRESS INDICATORS

ITEM R	DATE S

LIST KEY PERSONNEL POSITION	WEEKS ON PROJECT	SALARY/ WEEK	NO. OF CLIENTS SERVED
			COST PER CLIENT

COSTS REQUESTED FROM FUNDER ▶ U

DONATED COSTS ▶

TOTAL COSTS ▶ T

▼ % OF TOTAL
▼
▼
100%

INDIRECT COSTS AVAILABLE UNDER THE GRANT ARE: _____ % TDC x BOX T = _____ OR _____ % S & W x BOX U _____ =

223

PROJECT PLANNER ™

BAUER ASSOCIATES

PROJECT TITLE: Grants Coordination

PROJECT DIRECTOR: Research Coordinator

DATE: 12/88 to 14/89

OBJECTIVES (What are you going to accomplish?) A	ACTIVITIES • ACTION STEPS • METHODS (How will you do it?) B	DATE BEGIN/END C/D	WEEKS E	WHO (will do it?) F	PERSONNEL COSTS — SALARIES & WAGES G	FRINGE BENEFITS % OR $ H	TOTAL I	CONSULTANTS • CONTRACT SERVICES — WEEKS J	COST/WEEK K	TOTAL L	NON-PERSONNEL RESOURCES NEEDED SUPPLIES • EQUIPMENT • MATERIALS — ITEM M	COST/ITEM N	QUANTITY O	TOT COST P	SUB-TOTAL COST FOR ACTIVITY — TOTAL I.L.P Q	MILESTONES PROGRESS INDICATORS — ITEM R	DATE S
	areas of interests and needs to set-up goals for the Grants office (1 year, 2 year, 3 year). Include success rate, number of proposals allocated by area, time allocated by area and budget allocated by area.																
	b) Develop a long range research plan for the department.																
B. Contacting Funding Sources	B-1 Identify government sources and contract by telephone, letter and personal visit (1 to 2 trips a year)	1/12		Research Coordinator							Travel to Washington, D.C.: Roundtrip Airfare — Hotel 3 nights per trip — Per Diem per trip — Car, taxi, metro per trip	250 / 300 / 100 / 100	6 / 6 / 6 / 6	1,500 / 1,800 / 600 / 600			
	a) Start B-1 develop linkage system on existing funding sources. Start developing webbing and linkage with new funding sources. After identifying prospects, store contract information, identify state and federal sources for projects. Gather information on each funding source (mailing lists, newsletters, annual reports, etc.).																

LIST KEY PERSONNEL — POSITION	WEEKS ON PROJECT	SALARY/WEEK	NO. OF CLIENTS SERVED		COSTS REQUESTED FROM FUNDER ▲ DONATED COSTS ▲ TOTAL COSTS ▲	U				% OF TOTAL
			COST PER CLIENT					T		100%

INDIRECT COSTS AVAILABLE UNDER THE GRANT ARE: _____ % TDC x BOX T _____ = _____ OR _____ % S & W x BOX U _____ =

PROJECT TITLE: GRANTS COORDINATION   PROJECT DIRECTOR: RESEARCH COORDINATOR   DATE: _____

OBJECTIVES (What are you going to accomplish?) A	ACTIVITIES • ACTION STEPS • METHODS (How will you do it?) B	DATE BEGIN / END C/D	WEEKS E	WHO (which one?) F	PERSONNEL COSTS				CONSULTANTS • CONTRACT SERVICES				NON-PERSONNEL RESOURCES NEEDED SUPPLIES • EQUIPMENT • MATERIALS				SUB-TOTAL COST FOR ACTIVITY	MILESTONES PROGRESS INDICATORS		
					SALARIES & WAGES G	FRINGE BENEFITS % OR $ H	TOTAL I		WEEKS J	COST/WEEK K	TOTAL L	ITEM M	COST/ITEM N	QUANTITY O	TOT. COST P	TOTAL I.L.P Q	ITEM R	DATE S
	B-2 Identify foundations and corporations and contact by phone, letter and personal visit (4 trips/year). Integrate with Development office.	4/12		Research Coordinator								Travel re funding sources						
												Roundtrip airfare	200	4	800			
												Hotel Lodging per trip	100	4	400			
												Per Diem per trip	100	4	400			
	a) See "a" under B-1.											Car, taxi, subway per trip	50	4	200			
	b.																	
C. Proposal Preparation and submission	C-1 Assist in providing researchers with samples of funded proposals and the backgrounds of primary and secondary reviewers. Also provide the funding interests of the funding sources.	1/12		Research Coordinator														
	Assist in proposal development (size of budgets, negotiations as needed). Provide editorial assistance.																	
	C-2 Integrate proposals with existing grants system.	1/12		Research Coordinator														
D. Politics of Grant Seeking	D-1 Develop and maintain a webbing and linkage system with corporate, foundation and government funding sources.	1/12		Research Coordinator, Project Secretary, Staff members														
	D-2 Report to Chairperson on	1/12		Research Coordinator								Telephone Budget			1,200			

LIST KEY PERSONNEL POSITION	WEEKS ON PROJECT	SALARY/ WEEK	NO. OF CLIENTS SERVED		COST PER CLIENT

COSTS REQUESTED FROM FUNDER ▶
DONATED COSTS ▶
TOTAL COSTS ▶   U

INDIRECT COSTS AVAILABLE UNDER THE GRANT ARE: % TDC x BOX T = _____   OR _____ % S & W x BOX U = _____

% OF TOTAL ▼ ▼ ▼   100%
% TDC x BOX T = _____   OR _____ % S & W x BOX U _____ =

PROJECT PLANNER ™

BAUER ASSOCIATES

PROJECT TITLE: _GRANTS COORDINATION_   PROJECT DIRECTOR: _RESEARCH COORDINATOR_   DATE: _12/88 to 12/89_

OBJECTIVES (What are you going to accomplish?)	ACTIVITIES • ACTION STEPS • METHODS (How will you do it?)	DATE BEGIN C/D	DATE END	WEEKS E	WHO (will do it?) F	PERSONNEL COSTS				CONSULTANTS • CONTRACT SERVICES				NON-PERSONNEL RESOURCES NEEDED SUPPLIES • EQUIPMENT • MATERIALS					SUB-TOTAL COST FOR ACTIVITY	MILESTONES PROGRESS INDICATORS		
A	B					SALARIES & WAGES G	FRINGE BENEFITS % OR $ H	TOTAL I		WEEKS J	COST/WEEK K	TOTAL L		ITEM M	COST/ITEM N	QUANTITY O	TOT COST P	TOTAL I.L.P Q		ITEM R	DATE S
	political aspects of grant funding. This includes drafting letters, making telephone calls and sending telegrams to appropriate officials to influence funding.																				
E. Conferences, meetings and Training for Research Coordinator	E-1 Example: Attend American Society of Research Administrators' conference.	1/12			Research Coordinator									Airfare, hotel, meals and Registration fee per conference/ meeting							

COSTS REQUESTED FROM FUNDER ▲
DONATED COSTS ▲
TOTAL COSTS ▲

U

LIST KEY PERSONNEL	WEEKS ON PROJECT	NO. OF CLIENTS SERVED
POSITION	SALARY/ WEEK	
		COST PER CLIENT

100%

▼ ▼ ▼   % OF TOTAL

INDIRECT COSTS AVAILABLE UNDER THE GRANT ARE: ____ % TDC x BOX T ____ = ____ OR ____ % S & W x BOX U ____ =

226

JOB DESCRIPTION: DIRECTOR OF EXTRAMURAL FUNDING AND GRANTS MANAGEMENT

Responsibilities and Duties

Under the general direction of the director of the department, the director of extramural funding and grants management will perform duties necessary to accomplish the following broad objectives:

- increasing the interest and broadening participation of faculty/staff in the development of proposals for externally funded contracts and grants

- providing assistance to faculty/staff in the conceptualization, preparation, and processing of proposals

- establishing contacts with and collecting information from funding sources in both the public and private sectors

- disseminating in a timely manner and making conveniently available to faculty/staff information on funding opportunities, program guidelines, application materials, and other relevant information

- assisting in the formulation and implementation of a comprehensive plan for research and development that will help prioritize and enhance efforts to obtain external funding

- accomplishing various other tasks related to contract and grant development

Minimum Qualifications

Education: Master's degree from accredited institution preferred. Professional experience that demonstrates that the applicant has acquired and successfully applied the knowledge and abilities shown below may be substituted in lieu of the desired education requirement.

Experience: At least 3 years of cumulative, successful experience in all, or most, of the following areas:

1. writing grant proposals and competing for external funding
2. working with faculty and/or others to assist them on various aspects of contract and grant development
3. developing contacts with federal, state, local and private funding agencies
4. directing the development and operations of an office or program and supervising one or more staff persons

Knowledge and Abilities: General knowledge of the following aspects of contract and grant development:

1. sources of information on funding opportunities in both the public and private sectors
2. nature of externally funded research, training, and service programs in health and/or higher-education institutions
3. federal, state, and institutional policies and regulations governing externally funded programs
4. concepts and methods for preparing grant proposals and contracts
5. principles and methods of office and personnel management

Ability to assist faculty and staff in conceptualizing and developing grant proposals; ability to establish effective contacts with funding agencies; ability to supervise the work of both technical and clerical assistants; ability to develop good working relationships with faculty/staff; ability to creatively and independently plan, coordinate, and initiate actions necessary to implement administrative plans and decisions; and ability to communicate effectively both orally and in writing.

PROPOSAL- AND RESOURCE- DEVELOPMENT SPECIALIST

Information Assistance

For all practical purposes, proposals are developed by principal investigators with assistance possibly from their associates. However, proposals can be the result of information concerning prospective sources of funds for research in areas where the proposer has interests and capabilities. The present Information Systems Coordinator would assist the development specialists in this area.

Editorial Assistance

Such an individual would not necessarily be a professional writer but would provide editorial, photographic, graphical, typing, and reproduction services when needed. Assistance with the total office resources in tailoring faculty ideas to fit the interests of different sponsors.

Interdisciplinary Research

Many faculty and organizational units do not have the orientation or flexibility to perform interdisciplinary research successfully. Faculty are normally discipline-oriented or traditional in nature. Organizational units do not often provide the proper climate or organizational environment for interdisciplinary scholars. Individuals from different disciplines have little motivation to work together toward a common goal. The faculty director of an interdisciplinary project is critical, but much of the load may be shared by the office through proper coordination by the development specialist. Leadership, administrative ability, and the power of persuasion can greatly assist the faculty director of a team project.

Governmental Relations

Greater attention must be paid to the development of our relationships with federal, state, and local governmental agencies. Knowledge of the people and the programs of each agency is critical. The interaction of the program monitor of an agency with a faculty member at _____ is a key ingredient in any successful proposal effort. More than this, _____ as an entity needs to be aware of the growing edge of the present and future activities of all agencies. Concern must also be given to both the legislative and executive branches regarding science and technology. The development specialist would assist the office in coordination of efforts of the university in this area.

DIRECTOR OF CONTRACT AND GRANT DEVELOPMENT

Responsibilities and Duties

Under the general direction of the dean of Graduate Studies and Research, the director will perform duties necessary to accomplish the following broad objectives: a) increasing the interest and broadening the participation of faculty/staff in the development of proposals for externally funded contracts and grants; b) providing assistance to faculty/staff in the conceptualization, preparation, and processing of proposals; c) establishing contracts with and collecting information from funding sources in both the public and private sectors; d) disseminating in a timely manner and making conveniently available to faculty/staff information on funding opportunities, program guidelines, application materials, and other relevant information; e) assisting in the formulation and implementation of a comprehensive plan for research and development that will help prioritize and enhance efforts to obtain external funding; and f) accomplishing various other tasks related to contract and grant development.

Minimum Qualifications

Education: Master's degree from accredited institution required. A doctorate or equivalent is desired. Professional experience that demonstrates that the applicant has acquired and successfully applied the knowledge and abilities shown below may be substituted in lieu of the desired education on a year-for-year basis.

Experience: At least 3 years of cumulative, successful experience in all, or most, of the following areas: a) writing grant proposals and competing for external funding; b) working with faculty and/or others to assist them on various aspects of contract and grant development; c) developing contacts with federal, state, local, and private funding agencies; and d) directing the development and operations of an office or program while supervising one or more staff persons.

Knowledge and Abilities: General knowledge of the following aspects of contract and grant development: a) sources of information on funding opportunities in both the public and private sectors; b) nature of externally funded research, training, and service programs in institutions of higher education; c) federal, state, and institutional policies and regulations governing externally funded programs; d) concepts and methods for preparing grant proposals and contracts; and e) principles and methods of office and personnel management. Ability to assist faculty, staff, and students in conceptualizing and developing grant proposals; ability to establish effective contacts with funding agencies; ability to supervise the work of both technical and clerical assistants; ability to develop good working relationships with faculty, staff, and students; ability to creatively and independently plan, coordinate, and initiate actions necessary to implement administrative plans and decisions; and ability to communicate effectively both orally and in writing.

230

Index

David G. Bauer Associates, Inc.
2604 Elmwood Avenue
Suite 248
Rochester, New York 14618
(716) 271-5879

GRANTSEEKING MATERIALS

Order the following materials directly from Bauer Associates. *Please note that the prices do not include UPS shipping charges and are subject to change without notice.*

The "How To" Grants Manual - 229 pages of text, forms and worksheets to improve grantseeking skills. 2nd Edition.

$24.95
(+ shipping)

The Complete Grants Sourcebook for Higher Education - 465 pages of research on funding sources for higher education.

$85.00
(+ shipping)

The Complete Grants Sourcebook for Nursing and Health - A practical guide that includes an in-depth analysis of hundreds of funding sources for nursing and health.

$65.00
(+ shipping)

Proposal Organizing Workbook - Set of 30 Swiss Cheese Tabs

	Per Set	$ 9.95
10 or more sets	Per Set	$ 8.95
		(+ shipping)

Project Planner - Pad of 25 worksheets for developing your workplan and budget narrative.

	Per Pad	$ 8.95
10 or more pads	Per Pad	$ 7.95
		(+ shipping)

Grants Time Line - Pad of 25 worksheets for developing time lines and cash forecasts.

	Per Pad	$ 3.95
10 or more pads	Per Pad	$ 2.95
		(+ shipping)

Grant Winner - Software package of 4 diskettes for IBM-PC or compatible. Includes user's manual and a copy of The "How To" Grants Manual. Organizes grantseeking techniques and stores 4 proposals and worksheets in The "How To" Manual. $215.00. **To order call (703) 823-6966 M-F 9-5 Eastern Time, for more information call (619) 758-5213 M-F 9-5 Pacific Time.**

Winning Grants - Ten 1 hour videocassettes providing a systematic approach to developing a successful grant winning system. Sponsored by the American Council on Education and the University of Nebraska. $995.00. **To order, or for more information, call (619) 758-5213 M-F 9-5 Pacific Time.**

In-House Seminars - Use David Bauer to increase skills and interest in grantseeking at your institution or organization. Call Bauer Associates (716) 271-5879 for fee information and to find out when David is able to include you in his travel schedule.

234